50 Premium Cookie Recipes for Home

By: Kelly Johnson

Table of Contents

- Double Chocolate Chip Cookies
- Classic French Macarons
- Salted Caramel Pretzel Cookies
- Pistachio White Chocolate Cookies
- Lemon Lavender Shortbread
- Raspberry Almond Thumbprints
- Espresso Brownie Cookies
- Maple Pecan Cookies
- Coconut Lime Bars
- Ginger Molasses Cookies
- Peanut Butter Swirl Cookies
- Cherry Almond Biscotti
- S'mores Stuffed Cookies
- Chocolate Hazelnut Cookies
- Cinnamon Roll Cookies
- Orange Cardamom Cookies
- Toffee Walnut Cookies
- Dark Chocolate Sea Salt Cookies
- Pumpkin Spice Crinkle Cookies
- Saffron Pistachio Cookies
- Matcha White Chocolate Cookies
- Coconut Macaroons
- Brown Butter Bourbon Cookies
- Strawberry Cheesecake Cookies
- Caramel Pecan Turtle Cookies
- Mint Chocolate Chip Cookies
- Peach Cobbler Cookies
- Almond Joy Cookies
- Chai Spice Cookies
- Raspberry White Chocolate Oatmeal Cookies
- Blueberry Lemon Cookies
- Espresso Mocha Cookies
- Spiced Apple Cider Cookies
- Nutella-Stuffed Cookies
- Red Velvet Cookies
- Hibiscus Orange Cookies

- Gingerbread Whoopie Pies
- Peanut Butter Pretzel Cookies
- Nutty Biscotti
- Honey Walnut Cookies
- Pumpkin Chocolate Chip Cookies
- Cinnamon Sugar Stars
- Maple Bacon Cookies
- Tiramisu Cookies
- Cream Cheese Sugar Cookies
- Choco-Peanut Butter Swirl Cookies
- Mango Coconut Cookies
- Chili Chocolate Cookies
- S'mores Macarons
- Lemon Cream Sandwich Cookies

Double Chocolate Chip Cookies

Ingredients:

- **1 cup (2 sticks) unsalted butter**, at room temperature
- **1 cup granulated sugar**
- **1 cup packed brown sugar**
- **2 large eggs**
- **2 teaspoons vanilla extract**
- **2 1/4 cups all-purpose flour**
- **3/4 cup unsweetened cocoa powder**
- **1 teaspoon baking powder**
- **1/2 teaspoon baking soda**
- **1/2 teaspoon salt**
- **1 1/2 cups semisweet chocolate chips**
- **1 cup milk chocolate chips**

Instructions:

1. **Preheat Oven**: Preheat your oven to 350°F (175°C). Line baking sheets with parchment paper.
2. **Cream Butter and Sugars**: In a large bowl, beat the butter, granulated sugar, and brown sugar together until light and fluffy.
3. **Add Eggs and Vanilla**: Beat in the eggs one at a time, then mix in the vanilla extract.
4. **Combine Dry Ingredients**: In another bowl, whisk together the flour, cocoa powder, baking powder, baking soda, and salt.
5. **Mix Dry Ingredients with Wet Ingredients**: Gradually add the dry ingredients to the butter mixture, mixing just until combined.
6. **Stir in Chocolate Chips**: Fold in the semisweet and milk chocolate chips.
7. **Scoop Dough**: Drop rounded tablespoons of dough onto the prepared baking sheets, spacing them about 2 inches apart.
8. **Bake**: Bake for 10-12 minutes, or until the edges are set but the centers are still soft.
9. **Cool**: Let the cookies cool on the baking sheets for a few minutes before transferring them to a wire rack to cool completely.

Enjoy your rich, chocolatey double chocolate chip cookies!

Classic French Macarons

Ingredients:

For the Macaron Shells:

- **1 cup (120g) almond flour**
- **1 3/4 cups (220g) powdered sugar**
- **3 large egg whites**, at room temperature
- **1/4 teaspoon cream of tartar**
- **1/4 cup (50g) granulated sugar**
- **Gel food coloring** (optional)

For the Filling:

- **1/2 cup (115g) unsalted butter**, at room temperature
- **1 1/2 cups (190g) powdered sugar**
- **1 teaspoon vanilla extract**
- **1-2 tablespoons heavy cream** (adjust for desired consistency)

Instructions:

1. **Prepare Baking Sheets**: Line two baking sheets with parchment paper or silicone baking mats. You can also use a macaron template to ensure even-sized shells.
2. **Sift Dry Ingredients**: Sift together the almond flour and powdered sugar into a bowl. This helps to remove any lumps and ensures a smooth batter.
3. **Whip Egg Whites**: In a clean, dry bowl, beat the egg whites with an electric mixer on medium speed until foamy. Add the cream of tartar and continue to beat until soft peaks form. Gradually add the granulated sugar and continue to beat until stiff, glossy peaks form. If using food coloring, add it during this stage.
4. **Fold in Dry Ingredients**: Gently fold the sifted almond flour and powdered sugar into the meringue in thirds. Use a spatula to fold the mixture until just combined, making sure not to overmix. The batter should flow slowly off the spatula and form a ribbon.
5. **Pipe the Macarons**: Transfer the batter to a piping bag fitted with a round tip. Pipe circles of batter onto the prepared baking sheets, about 1.5 inches in diameter. Tap the baking sheets on the counter to release any air bubbles and flatten the tops slightly.
6. **Rest the Macarons**: Let the piped macarons sit at room temperature for 30-60 minutes, or until a skin forms on the surface. They should not stick to your finger when touched lightly.
7. **Preheat Oven**: While the macarons are resting, preheat your oven to 300°F (150°C).
8. **Bake**: Bake the macarons for 15-18 minutes, or until they have risen slightly and have a firm shell. They should not brown. Rotate the baking sheets halfway through baking for even results.
9. **Cool**: Allow the macarons to cool completely on the baking sheets before carefully removing them.

10. **Prepare the Filling**: Beat the butter until creamy. Gradually add the powdered sugar and continue to beat until light and fluffy. Mix in the vanilla extract. Adjust the consistency with heavy cream as needed.
11. **Assemble**: Pair up the macaron shells of similar sizes. Pipe or spread a small amount of filling on the flat side of one shell and top with another shell to create a sandwich.
12. **Mature the Macarons**: For best results, let the assembled macarons sit in the refrigerator for 24 hours to allow the flavors to meld and the texture to improve.

Enjoy your classic French macarons with their delicate, chewy texture and sweet filling!

Salted Caramel Pretzel Cookies

Ingredients:

For the Cookies:

- **1 cup (2 sticks) unsalted butter**, at room temperature
- **1 cup granulated sugar**
- **1 cup packed brown sugar**
- **2 large eggs**
- **1 teaspoon vanilla extract**
- **3 cups all-purpose flour**
- **1 teaspoon baking powder**
- **1/2 teaspoon baking soda**
- **1/2 teaspoon salt**
- **1 cup pretzel pieces** (about 2 cups pretzels, broken)
- **1 cup caramel bits** or chopped caramel candies
- **1/2 cup coarse sea salt**, for sprinkling

Optional:

- **1/2 cup chocolate chips** or chunks (for extra richness)

Instructions:

1. **Preheat Oven**: Preheat your oven to 350°F (175°C). Line baking sheets with parchment paper or silicone baking mats.
2. **Cream Butter and Sugars**: In a large bowl, beat the butter, granulated sugar, and brown sugar together until light and fluffy.
3. **Add Eggs and Vanilla**: Beat in the eggs one at a time, then mix in the vanilla extract.
4. **Combine Dry Ingredients**: In another bowl, whisk together the flour, baking powder, baking soda, and salt.
5. **Mix Dry Ingredients with Wet Ingredients**: Gradually add the dry ingredients to the butter mixture, mixing just until combined.
6. **Add Pretzels and Caramels**: Fold in the pretzel pieces and caramel bits (and chocolate chips if using).
7. **Scoop Dough**: Drop rounded tablespoons of dough onto the prepared baking sheets, spacing them about 2 inches apart. Press a few extra pretzel pieces and caramel bits onto the tops of the cookies if desired.
8. **Bake**: Bake for 10-12 minutes, or until the edges are golden and the centers are set.
9. **Add Sea Salt**: Immediately after removing the cookies from the oven, sprinkle the tops with coarse sea salt.
10. **Cool**: Let the cookies cool on the baking sheets for a few minutes before transferring them to a wire rack to cool completely.

These Salted Caramel Pretzel Cookies offer a delightful combination of sweet, salty, and crunchy flavors, perfect for satisfying a craving for something both indulgent and unique!

Pistachio White Chocolate Cookies

Ingredients:

- **1 cup (2 sticks) unsalted butter**, at room temperature
- **1 cup granulated sugar**
- **1 cup packed brown sugar**
- **2 large eggs**
- **1 teaspoon vanilla extract**
- **2 1/4 cups all-purpose flour**
- **1 teaspoon baking soda**
- **1/2 teaspoon salt**
- **1 cup shelled pistachios**, roughly chopped
- **1 cup white chocolate chips**

Instructions:

1. **Preheat Oven**: Preheat your oven to 350°F (175°C). Line baking sheets with parchment paper or silicone baking mats.
2. **Cream Butter and Sugars**: In a large bowl, beat the butter, granulated sugar, and brown sugar together until light and fluffy.
3. **Add Eggs and Vanilla**: Beat in the eggs one at a time, then mix in the vanilla extract.
4. **Combine Dry Ingredients**: In another bowl, whisk together the flour, baking soda, and salt.
5. **Mix Dry Ingredients with Wet Ingredients**: Gradually add the dry ingredients to the butter mixture, mixing just until combined.
6. **Add Pistachios and White Chocolate Chips**: Fold in the chopped pistachios and white chocolate chips.
7. **Scoop Dough**: Drop rounded tablespoons of dough onto the prepared baking sheets, spacing them about 2 inches apart.
8. **Bake**: Bake for 10-12 minutes, or until the edges are lightly golden and the centers are set.
9. **Cool**: Allow the cookies to cool on the baking sheets for a few minutes before transferring them to a wire rack to cool completely.

These Pistachio White Chocolate Cookies are a perfect blend of crunchy pistachios and creamy white chocolate, making them a delightful treat for any occasion!

Lemon Lavender Shortbread

Ingredients:

- **1 cup (2 sticks) unsalted butter**, at room temperature
- **1/2 cup granulated sugar**
- **1/4 cup powdered sugar**
- **2 tablespoons finely grated lemon zest** (about 2 lemons)
- **1 tablespoon dried culinary lavender** (make sure it's food-grade)
- **2 cups all-purpose flour**
- **1/4 teaspoon salt**
- **Optional: extra granulated sugar for sprinkling**

Instructions:

1. **Preheat Oven**: Preheat your oven to 325°F (165°C). Line baking sheets with parchment paper or silicone baking mats.
2. **Cream Butter and Sugars**: In a large bowl, beat the butter, granulated sugar, and powdered sugar together until light and fluffy.
3. **Add Lemon Zest and Lavender**: Mix in the lemon zest and dried lavender.
4. **Combine Dry Ingredients**: In another bowl, whisk together the flour and salt.
5. **Mix Dry Ingredients with Wet Ingredients**: Gradually add the dry ingredients to the butter mixture, mixing just until combined. The dough will be crumbly but should hold together when pressed.
6. **Form the Dough**: Turn the dough out onto a lightly floured surface and gently knead it a few times until it comes together. Roll out the dough to about 1/4 inch thickness.
7. **Cut Out Cookies**: Use a cookie cutter to cut out shapes from the dough, or cut it into squares or rectangles. Transfer the cut-out cookies to the prepared baking sheets.
8. **Optional**: If desired, sprinkle a small amount of granulated sugar on top of each cookie for extra sweetness and crunch.
9. **Bake**: Bake for 12-15 minutes, or until the edges are lightly golden. The centers should be set but not browned.
10. **Cool**: Allow the cookies to cool on the baking sheets for a few minutes before transferring them to a wire rack to cool completely.

These Lemon Lavender Shortbread cookies are a perfect combination of zesty lemon and aromatic lavender, making them a refreshing and elegant treat!

Raspberry Almond Thumbprints

Ingredients:

For the Cookies:

- **1 cup (2 sticks) unsalted butter**, at room temperature
- **1/2 cup granulated sugar**
- **1/2 cup packed brown sugar**
- **1 large egg yolk**
- **1 teaspoon vanilla extract**
- **2 cups all-purpose flour**
- **1/4 teaspoon salt**
- **1/2 cup finely chopped almonds** (toasted if desired)

For the Filling:

- **1/2 cup raspberry jam** (or any other berry jam of your choice)

Instructions:

1. **Preheat Oven**: Preheat your oven to 350°F (175°C). Line baking sheets with parchment paper or silicone baking mats.
2. **Cream Butter and Sugars**: In a large bowl, beat the butter, granulated sugar, and brown sugar together until light and fluffy.
3. **Add Egg Yolk and Vanilla**: Beat in the egg yolk and vanilla extract until well combined.
4. **Combine Dry Ingredients**: In another bowl, whisk together the flour and salt.
5. **Mix Dry Ingredients with Wet Ingredients**: Gradually add the dry ingredients to the butter mixture, mixing just until combined.
6. **Form Cookies**: Roll the dough into 1-inch balls and then roll each ball in the finely chopped almonds. Place the coated balls on the prepared baking sheets.
7. **Create Thumbprints**: Use your thumb or the back of a small spoon to make an indentation in the center of each cookie dough ball.
8. **Add Jam**: Fill each indentation with a small teaspoon of raspberry jam.
9. **Bake**: Bake for 12-15 minutes, or until the edges are lightly golden. The jam may bubble a bit, which is normal.
10. **Cool**: Allow the cookies to cool on the baking sheets for a few minutes before transferring them to a wire rack to cool completely.

These Raspberry Almond Thumbprint Cookies offer a delightful combination of buttery shortbread, crunchy almonds, and sweet, tangy raspberry jam—perfect for a delicious and elegant treat!

Espresso Brownie Cookies

Ingredients:

- **1/2 cup (1 stick) unsalted butter**, at room temperature
- **1 cup granulated sugar**
- **1/2 cup packed brown sugar**
- **2 large eggs**
- **1 teaspoon vanilla extract**
- **1/2 cup cocoa powder**
- **1 cup all-purpose flour**
- **1/2 teaspoon baking powder**
- **1/4 teaspoon salt**
- **2 tablespoons finely ground espresso** (or instant espresso powder)
- **1 cup semisweet chocolate chips** (or chunks)

Instructions:

1. **Preheat Oven**: Preheat your oven to 350°F (175°C). Line baking sheets with parchment paper or silicone baking mats.
2. **Cream Butter and Sugars**: In a large bowl, beat the butter, granulated sugar, and brown sugar together until light and fluffy.
3. **Add Eggs and Vanilla**: Beat in the eggs one at a time, then mix in the vanilla extract.
4. **Combine Dry Ingredients**: In another bowl, whisk together the cocoa powder, flour, baking powder, salt, and finely ground espresso.
5. **Mix Dry Ingredients with Wet Ingredients**: Gradually add the dry ingredients to the butter mixture, mixing just until combined.
6. **Fold in Chocolate Chips**: Stir in the chocolate chips or chunks.
7. **Scoop Dough**: Drop rounded tablespoons of dough onto the prepared baking sheets, spacing them about 2 inches apart.
8. **Bake**: Bake for 10-12 minutes, or until the edges are set and the centers are slightly soft. The cookies will continue to firm up as they cool.
9. **Cool**: Allow the cookies to cool on the baking sheets for a few minutes before transferring them to a wire rack to cool completely.

These Espresso Brownie Cookies offer a perfect blend of rich chocolate brownie texture and a robust coffee flavor, making them a delightful treat for both coffee and chocolate lovers!

Maple Pecan Cookies

Ingredients:

- **1 cup (2 sticks) unsalted butter**, at room temperature
- **1 cup granulated sugar**
- **1/2 cup packed brown sugar**
- **1/2 cup pure maple syrup** (preferably Grade A)
- **1 large egg**
- **1 teaspoon vanilla extract**
- **2 1/2 cups all-purpose flour**
- **1 teaspoon baking powder**
- **1/2 teaspoon baking soda**
- **1/4 teaspoon salt**
- **1 cup chopped pecans** (toasted if desired)
- **Optional: 1/4 cup coarse sugar** (for rolling or sprinkling)

Instructions:

1. **Preheat Oven**: Preheat your oven to 350°F (175°C). Line baking sheets with parchment paper or silicone baking mats.
2. **Cream Butter and Sugars**: In a large bowl, beat the butter, granulated sugar, and brown sugar together until light and fluffy.
3. **Add Maple Syrup, Egg, and Vanilla**: Beat in the maple syrup, egg, and vanilla extract until well combined.
4. **Combine Dry Ingredients**: In another bowl, whisk together the flour, baking powder, baking soda, and salt.
5. **Mix Dry Ingredients with Wet Ingredients**: Gradually add the dry ingredients to the butter mixture, mixing just until combined.
6. **Add Pecans**: Fold in the chopped pecans.
7. **Scoop Dough**: Drop rounded tablespoons of dough onto the prepared baking sheets, spacing them about 2 inches apart. If using, roll the dough balls in coarse sugar before placing them on the baking sheets.
8. **Bake**: Bake for 10-12 minutes, or until the edges are golden and the centers are set. The cookies should be soft in the middle.
9. **Cool**: Allow the cookies to cool on the baking sheets for a few minutes before transferring them to a wire rack to cool completely.

These Maple Pecan Cookies are a wonderful blend of sweet maple flavor and nutty pecans, perfect for a comforting and delicious treat!

Coconut Lime Bars

Ingredients:

For the Crust:

- 1 1/2 cups all-purpose flour
- 1/2 cup granulated sugar
- 1/2 cup unsalted butter, at room temperature
- 1/4 teaspoon salt

For the Filling:

- 1 cup granulated sugar
- 1/4 cup all-purpose flour
- 1/4 teaspoon baking powder
- 1/4 teaspoon salt
- 1/2 cup fresh lime juice (about 4-5 limes)
- 1 tablespoon lime zest (from about 2 limes)
- 3 large eggs
- 1 cup shredded coconut (sweetened or unsweetened, as preferred)

For the Topping (Optional):

- **Powdered sugar**, for dusting

Instructions:

1. **Preheat Oven**: Preheat your oven to 350°F (175°C). Line an 8x8-inch baking dish with parchment paper, leaving an overhang for easy removal.
2. **Prepare the Crust**: In a medium bowl, combine the flour, granulated sugar, and salt. Cut in the butter using a pastry cutter or your fingers until the mixture resembles coarse crumbs.
3. **Press the Crust**: Press the crust mixture evenly into the bottom of the prepared baking dish. Bake for 15-20 minutes, or until lightly golden.
4. **Prepare the Filling**: While the crust is baking, in a medium bowl, whisk together the granulated sugar, flour, baking powder, and salt. Add the lime juice, lime zest, and eggs, and whisk until well combined. Stir in the shredded coconut.
5. **Pour Filling**: Pour the filling over the pre-baked crust.
6. **Bake**: Bake for 25-30 minutes, or until the filling is set and the top is lightly golden. A toothpick inserted into the center should come out clean or with just a few moist crumbs.
7. **Cool**: Allow the bars to cool completely in the pan on a wire rack. Once cooled, use the parchment paper to lift the bars out of the pan and transfer them to a cutting board.
8. **Cut and Dust**: Cut into squares or bars. Dust with powdered sugar if desired before serving.

These Coconut Lime Bars offer a refreshing combination of tangy lime and sweet coconut, perfect for a light and tasty dessert!

Ginger Molasses Cookies

Ingredients:

- **3/4 cup (1 1/2 sticks) unsalted butter**, at room temperature
- **1 cup granulated sugar**, plus extra for rolling
- **1/2 cup packed brown sugar**
- **1/2 cup molasses**
- **1 large egg**
- **2 1/4 cups all-purpose flour**
- **2 teaspoons ground ginger**
- **1 teaspoon ground cinnamon**
- **1/2 teaspoon ground cloves**
- **1/2 teaspoon baking soda**
- **1/4 teaspoon salt**

Instructions:

1. **Preheat Oven**: Preheat your oven to 350°F (175°C). Line baking sheets with parchment paper or silicone baking mats.
2. **Cream Butter and Sugars**: In a large bowl, beat the butter, granulated sugar, and brown sugar together until light and fluffy.
3. **Add Molasses and Egg**: Mix in the molasses and egg until well combined.
4. **Combine Dry Ingredients**: In another bowl, whisk together the flour, ground ginger, ground cinnamon, ground cloves, baking soda, and salt.
5. **Mix Dry Ingredients with Wet Ingredients**: Gradually add the dry ingredients to the butter mixture, mixing just until combined.
6. **Form Cookies**: Roll rounded tablespoons of dough into balls and roll each ball in granulated sugar to coat. Place the coated dough balls on the prepared baking sheets, spacing them about 2 inches apart.
7. **Bake**: Bake for 10-12 minutes, or until the edges are set and the tops are cracked. The centers will still be soft but will firm up as they cool.
8. **Cool**: Allow the cookies to cool on the baking sheets for a few minutes before transferring them to a wire rack to cool completely.

These Ginger Molasses Cookies are perfect for enjoying with a cup of tea or coffee, with their spicy, sweet flavors and chewy texture.

Peanut Butter Swirl Cookies

Ingredients:

For the Peanut Butter Dough:

- **1 cup (2 sticks) unsalted butter**, at room temperature
- **1 cup creamy peanut butter**
- **1 cup granulated sugar**
- **1/2 cup packed brown sugar**
- **1 large egg**
- **1 teaspoon vanilla extract**
- **2 1/4 cups all-purpose flour**
- **1/2 teaspoon baking powder**
- **1/4 teaspoon baking soda**
- **1/4 teaspoon salt**

For the Chocolate Swirl:

- **1/2 cup semisweet chocolate chips**
- **2 tablespoons creamy peanut butter**

Instructions:

1. **Preheat Oven**: Preheat your oven to 350°F (175°C). Line baking sheets with parchment paper or silicone baking mats.
2. **Prepare Peanut Butter Dough**: In a large bowl, beat the butter, peanut butter, granulated sugar, and brown sugar together until creamy and light. Mix in the egg and vanilla extract until well combined.
3. **Combine Dry Ingredients**: In another bowl, whisk together the flour, baking powder, baking soda, and salt.
4. **Mix Dry Ingredients with Wet Ingredients**: Gradually add the dry ingredients to the peanut butter mixture, mixing until just combined.
5. **Prepare Chocolate Swirl**: In a small microwave-safe bowl, melt the chocolate chips and peanut butter together in the microwave, stirring every 20 seconds until smooth and combined.
6. **Create Swirls**: Drop rounded tablespoons of the peanut butter dough onto the prepared baking sheets. Use a small spoon or knife to create a swirl by drizzling a bit of the melted chocolate mixture on top of each dough ball and gently swirling it into the dough.
7. **Bake**: Bake for 10-12 minutes, or until the edges are set and the cookies are lightly golden. The centers may still look soft, but they will firm up as they cool.
8. **Cool**: Allow the cookies to cool on the baking sheets for a few minutes before transferring them to a wire rack to cool completely.

These Peanut Butter Swirl Cookies offer a delightful blend of rich peanut butter and smooth chocolate, perfect for satisfying your sweet tooth!

Cherry Almond Biscotti

Ingredients:

- **1 cup whole almonds**, toasted
- **1 cup dried cherries**, chopped
- **1 cup granulated sugar**
- **1/2 cup unsalted butter**, at room temperature
- **2 large eggs**
- **1 teaspoon vanilla extract**
- **1/2 teaspoon almond extract**
- **2 3/4 cups all-purpose flour**
- **2 teaspoons baking powder**
- **1/4 teaspoon salt**

Instructions:

1. **Preheat Oven**: Preheat your oven to 350°F (175°C). Line a baking sheet with parchment paper or a silicone baking mat.
2. **Prepare Almonds and Cherries**: Toast the almonds in a dry skillet over medium heat until fragrant and lightly browned, then let cool. Chop the dried cherries if they are large.
3. **Cream Butter and Sugar**: In a large bowl, cream the butter and granulated sugar together until light and fluffy.
4. **Add Eggs and Extracts**: Beat in the eggs one at a time, then mix in the vanilla extract and almond extract.
5. **Combine Dry Ingredients**: In another bowl, whisk together the flour, baking powder, and salt.
6. **Mix Dry Ingredients with Wet Ingredients**: Gradually add the dry ingredients to the butter mixture, mixing just until combined.
7. **Add Nuts and Cherries**: Fold in the toasted almonds and chopped cherries.
8. **Form Dough**: Divide the dough in half and shape each half into a log about 12 inches long and 2 inches wide on the prepared baking sheet. Flatten the logs slightly.
9. **Bake**: Bake for 25-30 minutes, or until the logs are golden brown and firm. Allow the logs to cool on the baking sheet for about 10 minutes.
10. **Slice and Second Bake**: Transfer the logs to a cutting board and use a serrated knife to slice them diagonally into 1/2-inch thick pieces. Arrange the slices cut side up on the baking sheet. Bake for an additional 10-15 minutes, turning the biscotti halfway through, until they are crisp and dry.
11. **Cool**: Let the biscotti cool completely on a wire rack.

These Cherry Almond Biscotti have a delightful crunch with a sweet and nutty flavor, making them a perfect treat to enjoy with a hot beverage!

S'mores Stuffed Cookies

Ingredients:

For the Cookie Dough:

- **1 cup (2 sticks) unsalted butter**, at room temperature
- **1 cup granulated sugar**
- **1 cup packed brown sugar**
- **2 large eggs**
- **1 teaspoon vanilla extract**
- **2 1/2 cups all-purpose flour**
- **1 teaspoon baking powder**
- **1 teaspoon baking soda**
- **1/2 teaspoon salt**

For the S'mores Filling:

- **1 cup mini marshmallows** (or about 8 large marshmallows, cut into small pieces)
- **1/2 cup graham cracker crumbs** (about 4-5 graham crackers, crushed)
- **1/2 cup chocolate chips** (semisweet or milk chocolate)

Instructions:

1. **Preheat Oven**: Preheat your oven to 350°F (175°C). Line baking sheets with parchment paper or silicone baking mats.
2. **Prepare Cookie Dough**: In a large bowl, beat the butter, granulated sugar, and brown sugar together until light and fluffy. Beat in the eggs one at a time, then mix in the vanilla extract.
3. **Combine Dry Ingredients**: In another bowl, whisk together the flour, baking powder, baking soda, and salt.
4. **Mix Dry Ingredients with Wet Ingredients**: Gradually add the dry ingredients to the butter mixture, mixing until just combined.
5. **Prepare the Filling**: In a small bowl, combine the mini marshmallows, graham cracker crumbs, and chocolate chips.
6. **Form Cookies**: Scoop out about 1.5 tablespoons of cookie dough and flatten it slightly in your palm. Place about 1 tablespoon of the s'mores filling in the center of the dough and then wrap the dough around the filling to seal it completely. Roll it into a ball and place it on the prepared baking sheet. Repeat with the remaining dough and filling, spacing the cookies about 2 inches apart.
7. **Bake**: Bake for 10-12 minutes, or until the edges are golden brown. The centers may look slightly underbaked; this is okay as they will continue to cook as they cool.
8. **Cool**: Allow the cookies to cool on the baking sheets for a few minutes before transferring them to a wire rack to cool completely.

These S'mores Stuffed Cookies are a delightful treat, combining the gooey goodness of s'mores with the chewy texture of a cookie. Enjoy them warm or at room temperature!

Chocolate Hazelnut Cookies

Ingredients:

- **1 cup (2 sticks) unsalted butter**, at room temperature
- **1 cup granulated sugar**
- **1 cup packed brown sugar**
- **2 large eggs**
- **1 teaspoon vanilla extract**
- **2 1/4 cups all-purpose flour**
- **1/2 cup unsweetened cocoa powder**
- **1 teaspoon baking soda**
- **1/2 teaspoon baking powder**
- **1/2 teaspoon salt**
- **1 cup semisweet chocolate chips**
- **1 cup chopped toasted hazelnuts** (see note for toasting instructions)

Instructions:

1. **Preheat Oven**: Preheat your oven to 350°F (175°C). Line baking sheets with parchment paper or silicone baking mats.
2. **Prepare Hazelnuts**: If your hazelnuts are not already toasted, spread them on a baking sheet and toast in the preheated oven for about 10 minutes, stirring occasionally, until fragrant and slightly darkened. Let them cool, then chop coarsely.
3. **Cream Butter and Sugars**: In a large bowl, beat the butter, granulated sugar, and brown sugar together until light and fluffy.
4. **Add Eggs and Vanilla**: Beat in the eggs one at a time, then mix in the vanilla extract until combined.
5. **Combine Dry Ingredients**: In another bowl, whisk together the flour, cocoa powder, baking soda, baking powder, and salt.
6. **Mix Dry Ingredients with Wet Ingredients**: Gradually add the dry ingredients to the butter mixture, mixing just until combined.
7. **Add Chocolate Chips and Hazelnuts**: Fold in the chocolate chips and chopped hazelnuts.
8. **Scoop Dough**: Drop rounded tablespoons of dough onto the prepared baking sheets, spacing them about 2 inches apart.
9. **Bake**: Bake for 10-12 minutes, or until the edges are set and the centers are slightly soft. The cookies will firm up as they cool.
10. **Cool**: Allow the cookies to cool on the baking sheets for a few minutes before transferring them to a wire rack to cool completely.

These Chocolate Hazelnut Cookies are a delightful combination of rich chocolate and nutty hazelnuts, offering a crunchy and flavorful treat that's sure to please any cookie lover!

Cinnamon Roll Cookies

Ingredients:

For the Cookie Dough:

- **1 cup (2 sticks) unsalted butter**, at room temperature
- 1 cup granulated sugar
- 1/2 cup packed brown sugar
- 2 large eggs
- 1 teaspoon vanilla extract
- 2 1/2 cups all-purpose flour
- 1 teaspoon baking powder
- 1/2 teaspoon baking soda
- 1/4 teaspoon salt

For the Cinnamon Filling:

- 1/2 cup granulated sugar
- 1 tablespoon ground cinnamon
- **2 tablespoons unsalted butter**, melted

For the Glaze:

- 1 cup powdered sugar
- 2-3 tablespoons milk
- 1/2 teaspoon vanilla extract

Instructions:

1. **Preheat Oven**: Preheat your oven to 350°F (175°C). Line baking sheets with parchment paper or silicone baking mats.
2. **Prepare the Cookie Dough**: In a large bowl, beat the butter, granulated sugar, and brown sugar together until light and fluffy. Beat in the eggs one at a time, then mix in the vanilla extract.
3. **Combine Dry Ingredients**: In another bowl, whisk together the flour, baking powder, baking soda, and salt.
4. **Mix Dry Ingredients with Wet Ingredients**: Gradually add the dry ingredients to the butter mixture, mixing until just combined.
5. **Prepare the Cinnamon Filling**: In a small bowl, mix together the granulated sugar and ground cinnamon. Stir in the melted butter until the mixture resembles a crumbly paste.
6. **Form Cookies**: Roll out the cookie dough on a lightly floured surface to about 1/4-inch thickness. Spread the cinnamon filling evenly over the dough. Roll the dough up into a log, starting from one edge. Slice the log into 1/2-inch thick rounds and place them on the prepared baking sheets.

7. **Bake**: Bake for 10-12 minutes, or until the edges are golden brown. The cookies will be soft in the center.
8. **Prepare the Glaze**: While the cookies are baking, whisk together the powdered sugar, milk, and vanilla extract until smooth. Adjust the milk to reach your desired consistency.
9. **Glaze the Cookies**: Allow the cookies to cool on the baking sheets for a few minutes before transferring them to a wire rack. Drizzle the glaze over the cooled cookies.

These Cinnamon Roll Cookies have a delightful cinnamon-sugar filling and a sweet glaze, making them a perfect treat for breakfast or a snack!

Orange Cardamom Cookies

Ingredients:

For the Cookies:

- **1 cup (2 sticks) unsalted butter**, at room temperature
- **1 cup granulated sugar**
- **1 large egg**
- **1 tablespoon finely grated orange zest** (about 1 orange)
- **2 teaspoons freshly ground cardamom**
- **2 1/4 cups all-purpose flour**
- **1/2 teaspoon baking powder**
- **1/4 teaspoon salt**

For the Glaze (Optional):

- **1 cup powdered sugar**
- **2-3 tablespoons fresh orange juice**
- **1/2 teaspoon vanilla extract**

Instructions:

1. **Preheat Oven**: Preheat your oven to 350°F (175°C). Line baking sheets with parchment paper or silicone baking mats.
2. **Cream Butter and Sugar**: In a large bowl, beat the butter and granulated sugar together until light and fluffy.
3. **Add Egg and Flavorings**: Beat in the egg, then mix in the orange zest and cardamom.
4. **Combine Dry Ingredients**: In another bowl, whisk together the flour, baking powder, and salt.
5. **Mix Dry Ingredients with Wet Ingredients**: Gradually add the dry ingredients to the butter mixture, mixing until just combined.
6. **Form Cookies**: Drop rounded tablespoons of dough onto the prepared baking sheets, spacing them about 2 inches apart. Flatten each dough ball slightly with the bottom of a glass or your hand.
7. **Bake**: Bake for 10-12 minutes, or until the edges are lightly golden and the centers are set. The cookies should be soft in the middle.
8. **Cool**: Allow the cookies to cool on the baking sheets for a few minutes before transferring them to a wire rack to cool completely.
9. **Prepare the Glaze (Optional)**: While the cookies are cooling, whisk together the powdered sugar, orange juice, and vanilla extract until smooth. Adjust the consistency with more orange juice or powdered sugar as needed.
10. **Glaze the Cookies**: Once the cookies are completely cool, drizzle the glaze over them.

These Orange Cardamom Cookies have a wonderful balance of zesty citrus and aromatic spice, making them a refreshing and sophisticated treat!

Toffee Walnut Cookies

Ingredients:

- **1 cup (2 sticks) unsalted butter**, at room temperature
- **1 cup granulated sugar**
- **1 cup packed brown sugar**
- **2 large eggs**
- **1 teaspoon vanilla extract**
- **2 1/4 cups all-purpose flour**
- **1 teaspoon baking soda**
- **1/2 teaspoon baking powder**
- **1/4 teaspoon salt**
- **1 cup toffee bits** (such as Heath Bits o' Brickle)
- **1 cup chopped walnuts** (toasted if desired)

Instructions:

1. **Preheat Oven**: Preheat your oven to 350°F (175°C). Line baking sheets with parchment paper or silicone baking mats.
2. **Cream Butter and Sugars**: In a large bowl, beat the butter, granulated sugar, and brown sugar together until light and fluffy.
3. **Add Eggs and Vanilla**: Beat in the eggs one at a time, then mix in the vanilla extract until combined.
4. **Combine Dry Ingredients**: In another bowl, whisk together the flour, baking soda, baking powder, and salt.
5. **Mix Dry Ingredients with Wet Ingredients**: Gradually add the dry ingredients to the butter mixture, mixing until just combined.
6. **Fold in Toffee and Walnuts**: Gently fold in the toffee bits and chopped walnuts.
7. **Form Cookies**: Drop rounded tablespoons of dough onto the prepared baking sheets, spacing them about 2 inches apart.
8. **Bake**: Bake for 10-12 minutes, or until the edges are lightly golden and the centers are set. The cookies will continue to firm up as they cool.
9. **Cool**: Allow the cookies to cool on the baking sheets for a few minutes before transferring them to a wire rack to cool completely.

These Toffee Walnut Cookies are a delightful treat with a satisfying crunch from the walnuts and a sweet, caramel-like flavor from the toffee bits. Perfect for a special occasion or a simple indulgence!

Dark Chocolate Sea Salt Cookies

Ingredients:

- **1 cup (2 sticks) unsalted butter**, at room temperature
- **1 cup granulated sugar**
- **1 cup packed brown sugar**
- **2 large eggs**
- **1 teaspoon vanilla extract**
- **2 1/4 cups all-purpose flour**
- **1/2 cup unsweetened cocoa powder**
- **1 teaspoon baking soda**
- **1/2 teaspoon baking powder**
- **1/4 teaspoon salt**
- **1 cup dark chocolate chips** (60% cacao or higher)
- **Coarse sea salt**, for sprinkling

Instructions:

1. **Preheat Oven**: Preheat your oven to 350°F (175°C). Line baking sheets with parchment paper or silicone baking mats.
2. **Cream Butter and Sugars**: In a large bowl, beat the butter, granulated sugar, and brown sugar together until light and fluffy.
3. **Add Eggs and Vanilla**: Beat in the eggs one at a time, then mix in the vanilla extract until combined.
4. **Combine Dry Ingredients**: In another bowl, whisk together the flour, cocoa powder, baking soda, baking powder, and salt.
5. **Mix Dry Ingredients with Wet Ingredients**: Gradually add the dry ingredients to the butter mixture, mixing until just combined.
6. **Fold in Dark Chocolate Chips**: Stir in the dark chocolate chips.
7. **Form Cookies**: Drop rounded tablespoons of dough onto the prepared baking sheets, spacing them about 2 inches apart. Lightly press down on each dough ball to flatten slightly.
8. **Bake**: Bake for 10-12 minutes, or until the edges are set and the centers are still slightly soft. The cookies will continue to firm up as they cool.
9. **Add Sea Salt**: As soon as the cookies come out of the oven, sprinkle a small pinch of coarse sea salt on top of each cookie.
10. **Cool**: Allow the cookies to cool on the baking sheets for a few minutes before transferring them to a wire rack to cool completely.

These Dark Chocolate Sea Salt Cookies have a rich chocolate flavor with a delightful crunch of sea salt, creating a sophisticated and delicious treat that's perfect for any occasion!

Pumpkin Spice Crinkle Cookies

Ingredients:

For the Cookies:

- **1 cup (2 sticks) unsalted butter**, at room temperature
- **1 cup granulated sugar**
- **1/2 cup packed brown sugar**
- **1 cup canned pumpkin puree** (not pumpkin pie filling)
- **2 large eggs**
- **1 teaspoon vanilla extract**
- **2 1/2 cups all-purpose flour**
- **2 teaspoons baking powder**
- **1 teaspoon baking soda**
- **1/2 teaspoon salt**
- **1 tablespoon pumpkin pie spice** (or a mix of cinnamon, nutmeg, and ginger)

For Rolling:

- **1/2 cup granulated sugar**
- **1/2 cup powdered sugar**

Instructions:

1. **Preheat Oven**: Preheat your oven to 350°F (175°C). Line baking sheets with parchment paper or silicone baking mats.
2. **Cream Butter and Sugars**: In a large bowl, beat the butter, granulated sugar, and brown sugar together until light and fluffy.
3. **Add Pumpkin, Eggs, and Vanilla**: Beat in the pumpkin puree, eggs, and vanilla extract until well combined.
4. **Combine Dry Ingredients**: In another bowl, whisk together the flour, baking powder, baking soda, salt, and pumpkin pie spice.
5. **Mix Dry Ingredients with Wet Ingredients**: Gradually add the dry ingredients to the butter mixture, mixing until just combined.
6. **Chill Dough**: For easier handling, chill the dough in the refrigerator for about 30 minutes.
7. **Prepare Rolling Mixture**: In a small bowl, combine the granulated sugar and powdered sugar.
8. **Form Cookies**: Scoop rounded tablespoons of dough and roll them into balls. Roll each ball in the sugar mixture to coat, then place them on the prepared baking sheets, spacing them about 2 inches apart.
9. **Bake**: Bake for 12-15 minutes, or until the edges are set and the cookies have crinkled and cracked on top. The centers should be soft.
10. **Cool**: Allow the cookies to cool on the baking sheets for a few minutes before transferring them to a wire rack to cool completely.

These Pumpkin Spice Crinkle Cookies are perfect for fall with their cozy pumpkin flavor and spicy warmth, and the powdered sugar coating gives them a lovely sweet touch!

Saffron Pistachio Cookies

Ingredients:

For the Cookies:

- **1 cup (2 sticks) unsalted butter**, at room temperature
- **1 cup granulated sugar**
- **1/2 cup powdered sugar**
- **1 large egg**
- **1 teaspoon vanilla extract**
- **2 1/4 cups all-purpose flour**
- **1/2 teaspoon baking powder**
- **1/4 teaspoon salt**
- **1/4 teaspoon ground cardamom** (optional, for added spice)
- **1/2 cup finely chopped pistachios**
- **A pinch of saffron threads** (about 1/4 teaspoon, soaked in 1 tablespoon warm milk)

For Garnish (Optional):

- **Whole pistachios**, for topping
- **Additional powdered sugar**, for dusting

Instructions:

1. **Preheat Oven**: Preheat your oven to 350°F (175°C). Line baking sheets with parchment paper or silicone baking mats.
2. **Cream Butter and Sugars**: In a large bowl, beat the butter, granulated sugar, and powdered sugar together until light and fluffy.
3. **Add Egg and Vanilla**: Beat in the egg and vanilla extract until well combined.
4. **Combine Dry Ingredients**: In another bowl, whisk together the flour, baking powder, salt, and ground cardamom (if using).
5. **Mix Dry Ingredients with Wet Ingredients**: Gradually add the dry ingredients to the butter mixture, mixing until just combined.
6. **Incorporate Saffron and Pistachios**: Gently fold in the chopped pistachios and the saffron threads along with the warm milk in which they were soaked.
7. **Form Cookies**: Scoop rounded tablespoons of dough and roll them into balls. Place them on the prepared baking sheets, spacing them about 2 inches apart. Flatten each ball slightly with the bottom of a glass or your hand. Press a whole pistachio into the center of each cookie, if using.
8. **Bake**: Bake for 10-12 minutes, or until the edges are lightly golden and the centers are set. The cookies will firm up as they cool.
9. **Cool and Dust**: Allow the cookies to cool on the baking sheets for a few minutes before transferring them to a wire rack to cool completely. Dust with additional powdered sugar if desired.

These Saffron Pistachio Cookies offer a luxurious and aromatic treat with the unique combination of saffron and pistachios. They're perfect for special occasions or to impress your guests with something a little different!

Matcha White Chocolate Cookies

Ingredients:

- **1 cup (2 sticks) unsalted butter**, at room temperature
- **1 cup granulated sugar**
- **1/2 cup packed brown sugar**
- **1 large egg**
- **1 teaspoon vanilla extract**
- **2 cups all-purpose flour**
- **2 tablespoons matcha powder** (culinary grade)
- **1 teaspoon baking powder**
- **1/2 teaspoon baking soda**
- **1/4 teaspoon salt**
- **1 cup white chocolate chips**

Instructions:

1. **Preheat Oven**: Preheat your oven to 350°F (175°C). Line baking sheets with parchment paper or silicone baking mats.
2. **Cream Butter and Sugars**: In a large bowl, beat the butter, granulated sugar, and brown sugar together until light and fluffy.
3. **Add Egg and Vanilla**: Beat in the egg and vanilla extract until well combined.
4. **Combine Dry Ingredients**: In another bowl, whisk together the flour, matcha powder, baking powder, baking soda, and salt.
5. **Mix Dry Ingredients with Wet Ingredients**: Gradually add the dry ingredients to the butter mixture, mixing until just combined.
6. **Fold in White Chocolate Chips**: Stir in the white chocolate chips until evenly distributed.
7. **Form Cookies**: Drop rounded tablespoons of dough onto the prepared baking sheets, spacing them about 2 inches apart. Flatten each dough ball slightly with the bottom of a glass or your hand.
8. **Bake**: Bake for 10-12 minutes, or until the edges are lightly golden and the centers are just set. The cookies will continue to firm up as they cool.
9. **Cool**: Allow the cookies to cool on the baking sheets for a few minutes before transferring them to a wire rack to cool completely.

These Matcha White Chocolate Cookies have a unique and vibrant flavor profile, with the matcha providing a lovely green color and a slightly earthy taste that pairs perfectly with the sweet, creamy white chocolate chips. Enjoy them with a cup of tea or as a special treat!

Coconut Macaroons

Ingredients:

- **4 large egg whites**
- **1 cup granulated sugar**
- **1/4 teaspoon salt**
- **1 teaspoon vanilla extract**
- **5 cups sweetened shredded coconut** (about 14 ounces)

For Dipping (Optional):

- **1 cup semisweet chocolate chips**
- **2 tablespoons coconut oil** (or vegetable oil)

Instructions:

1. **Preheat Oven**: Preheat your oven to 325°F (165°C). Line baking sheets with parchment paper or silicone baking mats.
2. **Beat Egg Whites**: In a large bowl, using an electric mixer, beat the egg whites on medium speed until they become frothy. Add the salt and continue beating until soft peaks form.
3. **Add Sugar and Vanilla**: Gradually add the granulated sugar, a little at a time, while continuing to beat until stiff peaks form. Mix in the vanilla extract.
4. **Fold in Coconut**: Gently fold the shredded coconut into the meringue mixture until well combined.
5. **Form Macaroons**: Drop rounded tablespoons of the mixture onto the prepared baking sheets, spacing them about 1 inch apart. You can use a small cookie scoop or two spoons to help shape the macaroons.
6. **Bake**: Bake for 15-20 minutes, or until the macaroons are golden brown and the edges are crisp. The centers should remain chewy.
7. **Cool**: Allow the macaroons to cool on the baking sheets for a few minutes before transferring them to a wire rack to cool completely.
8. **Optional Chocolate Dipping**: If desired, melt the chocolate chips and coconut oil together in a microwave-safe bowl or using a double boiler, stirring until smooth. Dip the bottom half of each macaroon into the melted chocolate, allowing excess chocolate to drip off. Place the dipped macaroons back on the parchment paper to set. You can also drizzle chocolate over the tops of the macaroons if preferred.
9. **Set and Store**: Let the chocolate set completely before storing. Store macaroons in an airtight container at room temperature for up to one week.

These Coconut Macaroons are deliciously sweet and chewy, with a hint of vanilla and the option of chocolate for a rich finish. Perfect for a special treat or as part of a holiday spread!

Brown Butter Bourbon Cookies

Ingredients:

For the Cookies:

- 1 cup (2 sticks) unsalted butter
- 1 cup granulated sugar
- 1 cup packed brown sugar
- 2 large eggs
- 1/4 cup bourbon
- 1 teaspoon vanilla extract
- 2 1/2 cups all-purpose flour
- 1 teaspoon baking powder
- 1/2 teaspoon baking soda
- 1/2 teaspoon salt
- 1 cup chopped pecans or walnuts (optional, for added texture)

For the Optional Glaze (if desired):

- 1 cup powdered sugar
- 2-3 tablespoons milk
- 1 tablespoon bourbon

Instructions:

1. **Brown the Butter**: In a medium saucepan over medium heat, melt the butter. Continue to cook, swirling the pan occasionally, until the butter foams and turns a deep golden brown with a nutty aroma. Be careful not to burn it. Remove from heat and let it cool slightly.
2. **Preheat Oven**: Preheat your oven to 350°F (175°C). Line baking sheets with parchment paper or silicone baking mats.
3. **Mix Sugars**: In a large bowl, combine the granulated sugar and brown sugar.
4. **Add Brown Butter and Eggs**: Pour the browned butter into the bowl with the sugars. Beat until well combined. Add the eggs one at a time, mixing well after each addition. Stir in the bourbon and vanilla extract.
5. **Combine Dry Ingredients**: In another bowl, whisk together the flour, baking powder, baking soda, and salt.
6. **Mix Dry Ingredients with Wet Ingredients**: Gradually add the dry ingredients to the butter mixture, mixing until just combined. If using, fold in the chopped nuts.
7. **Form Cookies**: Drop rounded tablespoons of dough onto the prepared baking sheets, spacing them about 2 inches apart.
8. **Bake**: Bake for 10-12 minutes, or until the edges are lightly golden and the centers are set. The cookies will firm up as they cool.
9. **Cool**: Allow the cookies to cool on the baking sheets for a few minutes before transferring them to a wire rack to cool completely.
10. **Optional Glaze**: If you'd like to add a glaze, whisk together the powdered sugar, milk, and bourbon until smooth. Drizzle the glaze over the cooled cookies.

These Brown Butter Bourbon Cookies have a rich, nutty flavor from the browned butter and a warm, complex depth from the bourbon, making them an elegant treat for any occasion!

Strawberry Cheesecake Cookies

Ingredients:

For the Cookies:

- **1 cup (2 sticks) unsalted butter**, at room temperature
- **1 cup granulated sugar**
- **1/2 cup packed brown sugar**
- **1 large egg**
- **1 teaspoon vanilla extract**
- **2 cups all-purpose flour**
- **1/2 teaspoon baking powder**
- **1/2 teaspoon baking soda**
- **1/4 teaspoon salt**
- **1 cup chopped fresh strawberries** (or frozen strawberries, thawed and drained)
- **1/2 cup finely crushed graham crackers** (for the cheesecake crust flavor)

For the Cream Cheese Filling:

- **4 ounces cream cheese**, softened
- **1/4 cup granulated sugar**
- **1/2 teaspoon vanilla extract**

Instructions:

1. **Preheat Oven**: Preheat your oven to 350°F (175°C). Line baking sheets with parchment paper or silicone baking mats.
2. **Prepare the Cream Cheese Filling**: In a small bowl, beat the cream cheese, granulated sugar, and vanilla extract until smooth and creamy. Chill in the refrigerator while you prepare the cookie dough.
3. **Cream Butter and Sugars**: In a large bowl, beat the butter, granulated sugar, and brown sugar together until light and fluffy.
4. **Add Egg and Vanilla**: Beat in the egg and vanilla extract until well combined.
5. **Combine Dry Ingredients**: In another bowl, whisk together the flour, baking powder, baking soda, and salt.
6. **Mix Dry Ingredients with Wet Ingredients**: Gradually add the dry ingredients to the butter mixture, mixing until just combined.
7. **Add Strawberries and Graham Cracker Crumbs**: Gently fold in the chopped strawberries and crushed graham crackers.
8. **Form Cookies**: Drop rounded tablespoons of dough onto the prepared baking sheets, spacing them about 2 inches apart. Use your thumb or the back of a spoon to make a small indentation in the center of each cookie.
9. **Add Cream Cheese Filling**: Place a small spoonful of the chilled cream cheese filling into the indentation of each cookie.
10. **Bake**: Bake for 12-15 minutes, or until the edges are lightly golden and the centers are set. The cream cheese filling should be slightly melted but not overcooked.
11. **Cool**: Allow the cookies to cool on the baking sheets for a few minutes before transferring them to a wire rack to cool completely.

These Strawberry Cheesecake Cookies combine the sweetness of strawberries with the rich, creamy flavor of cheesecake, all nestled in a cookie. They're perfect for a special treat or to impress your guests with something a bit different!

Caramel Pecan Turtle Cookies

Ingredients:

For the Cookies:

- **1 cup (2 sticks) unsalted butter**, at room temperature
- **1 cup granulated sugar**
- **1 cup packed brown sugar**
- **2 large eggs**
- **1 teaspoon vanilla extract**
- **2 1/2 cups all-purpose flour**
- **1 teaspoon baking powder**
- **1/2 teaspoon baking soda**
- **1/4 teaspoon salt**

For the Caramel:

- **1 cup soft caramel candies**, chopped (or store-bought caramel sauce)

For the Pecan Topping:

- **1 cup chopped pecans** (toasted if desired)

For Drizzling (Optional):

- **1/2 cup semisweet chocolate chips**
- **1 tablespoon coconut oil** (or vegetable oil)

Instructions:

1. **Preheat Oven**: Preheat your oven to 350°F (175°C). Line baking sheets with parchment paper or silicone baking mats.
2. **Prepare Cookie Dough**: In a large bowl, beat the butter, granulated sugar, and brown sugar together until light and fluffy. Beat in the eggs one at a time, then mix in the vanilla extract.
3. **Combine Dry Ingredients**: In another bowl, whisk together the flour, baking powder, baking soda, and salt.
4. **Mix Dry Ingredients with Wet Ingredients**: Gradually add the dry ingredients to the butter mixture, mixing until just combined.
5. **Form Cookies**: Scoop rounded tablespoons of dough and place them onto the prepared baking sheets, spacing them about 2 inches apart. Press a small piece of caramel into the center of each cookie dough ball, then gently press down to slightly flatten the dough.
6. **Add Pecan Topping**: Sprinkle chopped pecans on top of each cookie, pressing them lightly into the dough.
7. **Bake**: Bake for 12-15 minutes, or until the edges are lightly golden and the centers are set. The caramel will be soft and gooey inside the cookies.
8. **Cool**: Allow the cookies to cool on the baking sheets for a few minutes before transferring them to a wire rack to cool completely.

9. **Optional Chocolate Drizzle**: If you want to add a chocolate drizzle, melt the chocolate chips and coconut oil together in a microwave-safe bowl or using a double boiler, stirring until smooth. Drizzle the melted chocolate over the cooled cookies.

These Caramel Pecan Turtle Cookies offer a delightful combination of chewy caramel, crunchy pecans, and a rich cookie base, with an optional chocolate drizzle for extra indulgence. They're a perfect treat for any occasion!

Mint Chocolate Chip Cookies

Ingredients:

- **1 cup (2 sticks) unsalted butter**, at room temperature
- **1 cup granulated sugar**
- **1 cup packed brown sugar**
- **2 large eggs**
- **1 teaspoon vanilla extract**
- **1 teaspoon peppermint extract** (adjust to taste)
- **2 1/4 cups all-purpose flour**
- **1/2 teaspoon baking powder**
- **1/2 teaspoon baking soda**
- **1/4 teaspoon salt**
- **1 cup semisweet chocolate chips**
- **1/2 cup mini chocolate chips** (optional, for extra chocolatey goodness)
- **Green food coloring** (optional, for a minty green hue)

Instructions:

1. **Preheat Oven**: Preheat your oven to 350°F (175°C). Line baking sheets with parchment paper or silicone baking mats.
2. **Cream Butter and Sugars**: In a large bowl, beat the butter, granulated sugar, and brown sugar together until light and fluffy.
3. **Add Eggs and Extracts**: Beat in the eggs one at a time, then mix in the vanilla extract and peppermint extract. If using, add a few drops of green food coloring to achieve your desired minty green color.
4. **Combine Dry Ingredients**: In another bowl, whisk together the flour, baking powder, baking soda, and salt.
5. **Mix Dry Ingredients with Wet Ingredients**: Gradually add the dry ingredients to the butter mixture, mixing until just combined.
6. **Fold in Chocolate Chips**: Stir in the semisweet chocolate chips and mini chocolate chips (if using).
7. **Form Cookies**: Drop rounded tablespoons of dough onto the prepared baking sheets, spacing them about 2 inches apart. You can also use a cookie scoop for even-sized cookies.
8. **Bake**: Bake for 10-12 minutes, or until the edges are lightly golden and the centers are set. The cookies will firm up as they cool.
9. **Cool**: Allow the cookies to cool on the baking sheets for a few minutes before transferring them to a wire rack to cool completely.

These Mint Chocolate Chip Cookies are perfect for mint lovers, offering a refreshing minty flavor complemented by rich chocolate chips. They're great for any time of the year but especially festive around the holidays!

Peach Cobbler Cookies

Ingredients:

For the Cookies:

- **1 cup (2 sticks) unsalted butter**, at room temperature
- **1 cup granulated sugar**
- **1/2 cup packed brown sugar**
- **1 large egg**
- **1 teaspoon vanilla extract**
- **2 1/2 cups all-purpose flour**
- **1 teaspoon baking powder**
- **1/2 teaspoon baking soda**
- **1/4 teaspoon salt**
- **1 teaspoon ground cinnamon**
- **1/2 teaspoon ground nutmeg**
- **1 cup diced fresh peaches** (or frozen peaches, thawed and drained)
- **1/2 cup chopped pecans** (optional, for added texture)

For the Peach Filling (Optional):

- **1/2 cup peach preserves** or peach jam

For the Topping (Optional):

- **1/4 cup granulated sugar**
- **1 teaspoon ground cinnamon**

Instructions:

1. **Preheat Oven**: Preheat your oven to 350°F (175°C). Line baking sheets with parchment paper or silicone baking mats.
2. **Cream Butter and Sugars**: In a large bowl, beat the butter, granulated sugar, and brown sugar together until light and fluffy.
3. **Add Egg and Vanilla**: Beat in the egg and vanilla extract until well combined.
4. **Combine Dry Ingredients**: In another bowl, whisk together the flour, baking powder, baking soda, salt, cinnamon, and nutmeg.
5. **Mix Dry Ingredients with Wet Ingredients**: Gradually add the dry ingredients to the butter mixture, mixing until just combined. Fold in the diced peaches and chopped pecans (if using).
6. **Form Cookies**: Drop rounded tablespoons of dough onto the prepared baking sheets, spacing them about 2 inches apart. If using, place a small dollop of peach preserves or jam in the center of each cookie dough ball and gently press down to slightly flatten the dough.
7. **Add Topping (Optional)**: Mix the granulated sugar and cinnamon together. Sprinkle a small amount of this mixture on top of each cookie before baking.
8. **Bake**: Bake for 12-15 minutes, or until the edges are lightly golden and the centers are set. The cookies will firm up as they cool.

9. **Cool**: Allow the cookies to cool on the baking sheets for a few minutes before transferring them to a wire rack to cool completely.

These Peach Cobbler Cookies have the comforting flavors of peach cobbler in a cookie form, with optional peach preserves for extra sweetness and a sprinkle of cinnamon sugar for a touch of spice. Perfect for enjoying the taste of summer anytime!

Almond Joy Cookies

Ingredients:

For the Cookies:

- **1 cup (2 sticks) unsalted butter**, at room temperature
- 1 cup granulated sugar
- 1 cup packed brown sugar
- 2 large eggs
- 1 teaspoon vanilla extract
- 2 1/4 cups all-purpose flour
- 1/2 teaspoon baking powder
- 1/2 teaspoon baking soda
- 1/4 teaspoon salt
- 1 cup sweetened shredded coconut
- 1 cup chopped almonds
- 1 cup semisweet chocolate chips

For the Topping (Optional):

- 1/2 cup semisweet chocolate chips
- **1 tablespoon coconut oil** (or vegetable oil)

Instructions:

1. **Preheat Oven**: Preheat your oven to 350°F (175°C). Line baking sheets with parchment paper or silicone baking mats.
2. **Cream Butter and Sugars**: In a large bowl, beat the butter, granulated sugar, and brown sugar together until light and fluffy.
3. **Add Eggs and Vanilla**: Beat in the eggs one at a time, then mix in the vanilla extract.
4. **Combine Dry Ingredients**: In another bowl, whisk together the flour, baking powder, baking soda, and salt.
5. **Mix Dry Ingredients with Wet Ingredients**: Gradually add the dry ingredients to the butter mixture, mixing until just combined.
6. **Fold in Coconut, Almonds, and Chocolate Chips**: Gently fold in the shredded coconut, chopped almonds, and chocolate chips.
7. **Form Cookies**: Drop rounded tablespoons of dough onto the prepared baking sheets, spacing them about 2 inches apart. Press down lightly to slightly flatten each dough ball.
8. **Bake**: Bake for 10-12 minutes, or until the edges are golden and the centers are set. The cookies will firm up as they cool.
9. **Cool**: Allow the cookies to cool on the baking sheets for a few minutes before transferring them to a wire rack to cool completely.
10. **Optional Chocolate Drizzle**: If desired, melt the chocolate chips and coconut oil together in a microwave-safe bowl or using a double boiler, stirring until smooth. Drizzle the melted chocolate over the cooled cookies.

These Almond Joy Cookies bring together the classic flavors of the Almond Joy candy bar into a chewy, chocolatey cookie with crunchy almonds and sweet coconut. Enjoy them as a treat or share them with friends and family!

Chai Spice Cookies

Ingredients:

For the Cookies:

- **1 cup (2 sticks) unsalted butter**, at room temperature
- 1 cup granulated sugar
- 1/2 cup packed brown sugar
- 1 large egg
- 1 teaspoon vanilla extract
- 2 1/4 cups all-purpose flour
- 1 teaspoon baking powder
- 1/2 teaspoon baking soda
- 1/4 teaspoon salt

For the Chai Spice Blend:

- 1 teaspoon ground cinnamon
- 1/2 teaspoon ground ginger
- 1/2 teaspoon ground cardamom
- 1/4 teaspoon ground cloves
- 1/4 teaspoon ground black pepper

For Rolling (Optional):

- 1/4 cup granulated sugar
- 1 teaspoon ground cinnamon

Instructions:

1. **Preheat Oven**: Preheat your oven to 350°F (175°C). Line baking sheets with parchment paper or silicone baking mats.
2. **Prepare Chai Spice Blend**: In a small bowl, whisk together the ground cinnamon, ground ginger, ground cardamom, ground cloves, and ground black pepper.
3. **Cream Butter and Sugars**: In a large bowl, beat the butter, granulated sugar, and brown sugar together until light and fluffy.
4. **Add Egg and Vanilla**: Beat in the egg and vanilla extract until well combined.
5. **Combine Dry Ingredients**: In another bowl, whisk together the flour, baking powder, baking soda, salt, and the prepared chai spice blend.
6. **Mix Dry Ingredients with Wet Ingredients**: Gradually add the dry ingredients to the butter mixture, mixing until just combined.
7. **Form Cookies**: Drop rounded tablespoons of dough onto the prepared baking sheets, spacing them about 2 inches apart. For a more uniform shape, you can roll the dough into balls.
8. **Optional Rolling**: If you prefer, roll the cookie dough balls in a mixture of granulated sugar and ground cinnamon before placing them on the baking sheets.
9. **Bake**: Bake for 10-12 minutes, or until the edges are lightly golden and the centers are set. The cookies will firm up as they cool.

10. **Cool**: Allow the cookies to cool on the baking sheets for a few minutes before transferring them to a wire rack to cool completely.

These Chai Spice Cookies offer a delightful mix of warm spices, making them a cozy and flavorful treat. They pair wonderfully with a cup of tea or coffee, perfect for enjoying on a cool day or sharing with friends and family!

Raspberry White Chocolate Oatmeal Cookies

Ingredients:

- **1 cup (2 sticks) unsalted butter**, at room temperature
- **1 cup granulated sugar**
- **1/2 cup packed brown sugar**
- **2 large eggs**
- **1 teaspoon vanilla extract**
- **1 1/2 cups all-purpose flour**
- **1 teaspoon baking powder**
- **1/2 teaspoon baking soda**
- **1/4 teaspoon salt**
- **2 cups old-fashioned rolled oats**
- **1 cup white chocolate chips**
- **1 cup fresh raspberries** (or frozen raspberries, thawed and drained)

Instructions:

1. **Preheat Oven**: Preheat your oven to 350°F (175°C). Line baking sheets with parchment paper or silicone baking mats.
2. **Cream Butter and Sugars**: In a large bowl, beat the butter, granulated sugar, and brown sugar together until light and fluffy.
3. **Add Eggs and Vanilla**: Beat in the eggs one at a time, then mix in the vanilla extract.
4. **Combine Dry Ingredients**: In another bowl, whisk together the flour, baking powder, baking soda, and salt.
5. **Mix Dry Ingredients with Wet Ingredients**: Gradually add the dry ingredients to the butter mixture, mixing until just combined.
6. **Fold in Oats, White Chocolate, and Raspberries**: Stir in the rolled oats and white chocolate chips. Gently fold in the fresh raspberries. Be careful not to over-mix to avoid breaking up the raspberries too much.
7. **Form Cookies**: Drop rounded tablespoons of dough onto the prepared baking sheets, spacing them about 2 inches apart. The dough will be thick and chunky.
8. **Bake**: Bake for 12-15 minutes, or until the edges are lightly golden and the centers are set. The cookies will firm up as they cool.
9. **Cool**: Allow the cookies to cool on the baking sheets for a few minutes before transferring them to a wire rack to cool completely.

These Raspberry White Chocolate Oatmeal Cookies combine the chewy texture of oatmeal with the creamy sweetness of white chocolate and the bright, tart flavor of raspberries. They make for a delightful treat that's perfect for any time of year!

Blueberry Lemon Cookies

Ingredients:

- **1 cup (2 sticks) unsalted butter**, at room temperature
- **1 cup granulated sugar**
- **1/2 cup packed brown sugar**
- **1 large egg**
- **1 tablespoon lemon zest** (about 1 lemon)
- **2 tablespoons lemon juice** (about 1 lemon)
- **1 teaspoon vanilla extract**
- **2 1/4 cups all-purpose flour**
- **1 teaspoon baking powder**
- **1/2 teaspoon baking soda**
- **1/4 teaspoon salt**
- **1 cup fresh blueberries** (or frozen blueberries, thawed and drained)

For the Glaze (Optional):

- **1 cup powdered sugar**
- **2-3 tablespoons lemon juice**
- **1 teaspoon lemon zest**

Instructions:

1. **Preheat Oven**: Preheat your oven to 350°F (175°C). Line baking sheets with parchment paper or silicone baking mats.
2. **Cream Butter and Sugars**: In a large bowl, beat the butter, granulated sugar, and brown sugar together until light and fluffy.
3. **Add Egg and Flavorings**: Beat in the egg, lemon zest, lemon juice, and vanilla extract until well combined.
4. **Combine Dry Ingredients**: In another bowl, whisk together the flour, baking powder, baking soda, and salt.
5. **Mix Dry Ingredients with Wet Ingredients**: Gradually add the dry ingredients to the butter mixture, mixing until just combined.
6. **Fold in Blueberries**: Gently fold in the blueberries, being careful not to overmix to avoid breaking them up too much.
7. **Form Cookies**: Drop rounded tablespoons of dough onto the prepared baking sheets, spacing them about 2 inches apart. The dough will be soft and chunky.
8. **Bake**: Bake for 12-15 minutes, or until the edges are lightly golden and the centers are set. The cookies will firm up as they cool.
9. **Cool**: Allow the cookies to cool on the baking sheets for a few minutes before transferring them to a wire rack to cool completely.
10. **Optional Glaze**: If you'd like to add a glaze, whisk together the powdered sugar, lemon juice, and lemon zest until smooth. Drizzle the glaze over the cooled cookies.

These Blueberry Lemon Cookies have a delightful balance of tangy lemon and sweet blueberries, making them a refreshing and delicious treat. Enjoy them fresh with a cup of tea or as a special dessert!

Espresso Mocha Cookies

Ingredients:

- **1 cup (2 sticks) unsalted butter**, at room temperature
- **1 cup granulated sugar**
- **1 cup packed brown sugar**
- **2 large eggs**
- **1 teaspoon vanilla extract**
- **1 tablespoon instant espresso powder**
- **1/4 cup cocoa powder** (unsweetened)
- **2 1/4 cups all-purpose flour**
- **1 teaspoon baking powder**
- **1/2 teaspoon baking soda**
- **1/4 teaspoon salt**
- **1 cup semisweet chocolate chips**

Instructions:

1. **Preheat Oven**: Preheat your oven to 350°F (175°C). Line baking sheets with parchment paper or silicone baking mats.
2. **Cream Butter and Sugars**: In a large bowl, beat the butter, granulated sugar, and brown sugar together until light and fluffy.
3. **Add Eggs and Flavorings**: Beat in the eggs one at a time, then mix in the vanilla extract, instant espresso powder, and cocoa powder until well combined.
4. **Combine Dry Ingredients**: In another bowl, whisk together the flour, baking powder, baking soda, and salt.
5. **Mix Dry Ingredients with Wet Ingredients**: Gradually add the dry ingredients to the butter mixture, mixing until just combined.
6. **Fold in Chocolate Chips**: Stir in the semisweet chocolate chips.
7. **Form Cookies**: Drop rounded tablespoons of dough onto the prepared baking sheets, spacing them about 2 inches apart. You can use a cookie scoop for even-sized cookies.
8. **Bake**: Bake for 10-12 minutes, or until the edges are set and the centers are just beginning to firm up. The cookies will continue to cook slightly as they cool.
9. **Cool**: Allow the cookies to cool on the baking sheets for a few minutes before transferring them to a wire rack to cool completely.

These Espresso Mocha Cookies are perfect for coffee and chocolate lovers, offering a rich, bold flavor with a hint of espresso and plenty of chocolatey goodness. Enjoy them with a cup of coffee or as a special treat!

Spiced Apple Cider Cookies

Ingredients:

For the Cookies:

- **1 cup (2 sticks) unsalted butter**, at room temperature
- **1 cup granulated sugar**
- **1/2 cup packed brown sugar**
- **1 large egg**
- **1 teaspoon vanilla extract**
- **1/4 cup apple cider** (reduce slightly if using concentrate)
- **2 1/2 cups all-purpose flour**
- **1 teaspoon ground cinnamon**
- **1/2 teaspoon ground nutmeg**
- **1/2 teaspoon ground ginger**
- **1/2 teaspoon baking powder**
- **1/2 teaspoon baking soda**
- **1/4 teaspoon salt**

For the Optional Cinnamon Sugar Coating:

- **1/4 cup granulated sugar**
- **1 teaspoon ground cinnamon**

Instructions:

1. **Preheat Oven**: Preheat your oven to 350°F (175°C). Line baking sheets with parchment paper or silicone baking mats.
2. **Cream Butter and Sugars**: In a large bowl, beat the butter, granulated sugar, and brown sugar together until light and fluffy.
3. **Add Egg and Flavorings**: Beat in the egg, vanilla extract, and apple cider until well combined.
4. **Combine Dry Ingredients**: In another bowl, whisk together the flour, ground cinnamon, ground nutmeg, ground ginger, baking powder, baking soda, and salt.
5. **Mix Dry Ingredients with Wet Ingredients**: Gradually add the dry ingredients to the butter mixture, mixing until just combined.
6. **Form Cookies**: Drop rounded tablespoons of dough onto the prepared baking sheets, spacing them about 2 inches apart. If you prefer, roll the dough balls in a mixture of granulated sugar and ground cinnamon before placing them on the baking sheets for extra flavor and a sweet, spiced coating.
7. **Bake**: Bake for 10-12 minutes, or until the edges are lightly golden and the centers are set. The cookies will firm up as they cool.
8. **Cool**: Allow the cookies to cool on the baking sheets for a few minutes before transferring them to a wire rack to cool completely.

These Spiced Apple Cider Cookies have a wonderful blend of autumn spices and the subtle sweetness of apple cider, making them perfect for fall or any time you want a cozy, spiced treat. Enjoy them with a cup of tea or hot cider!

Nutella-Stuffed Cookies

Ingredients:

For the Cookies:

- **1 cup (2 sticks) unsalted butter**, at room temperature
- **1 cup granulated sugar**
- **1 cup packed brown sugar**
- **2 large eggs**
- **1 teaspoon vanilla extract**
- **2 1/4 cups all-purpose flour**
- **1/2 teaspoon baking powder**
- **1/2 teaspoon baking soda**
- **1/4 teaspoon salt**
- **1 cup semisweet chocolate chips** (optional, for extra chocolatey goodness)

For the Nutella Filling:

- **1/2 cup Nutella** (or other hazelnut spread)

Instructions:

1. **Prepare Nutella Filling**: Scoop out 1/2 teaspoon-sized portions of Nutella onto a parchment-lined tray or plate. Freeze for at least 30 minutes, or until firm. This helps keep the Nutella from melting too quickly during baking.
2. **Preheat Oven**: Preheat your oven to 350°F (175°C). Line baking sheets with parchment paper or silicone baking mats.
3. **Cream Butter and Sugars**: In a large bowl, beat the butter, granulated sugar, and brown sugar together until light and fluffy.
4. **Add Eggs and Vanilla**: Beat in the eggs one at a time, then mix in the vanilla extract.
5. **Combine Dry Ingredients**: In another bowl, whisk together the flour, baking powder, baking soda, and salt.
6. **Mix Dry Ingredients with Wet Ingredients**: Gradually add the dry ingredients to the butter mixture, mixing until just combined. If using, fold in the chocolate chips.
7. **Form Cookies**: Scoop out 1.5 tablespoons of cookie dough and flatten it slightly in your hand. Place a frozen Nutella ball in the center and wrap the dough around it, sealing the Nutella inside. Roll the dough into a ball and place it on the prepared baking sheet. Repeat with the remaining dough and Nutella.
8. **Bake**: Bake for 12-15 minutes, or until the edges are lightly golden and the centers are set. The cookies will spread slightly, creating a gooey center of Nutella.
9. **Cool**: Allow the cookies to cool on the baking sheets for a few minutes before transferring them to a wire rack to cool completely.

These Nutella-Stuffed Cookies are a decadent treat, with a gooey Nutella center hidden inside a soft and chewy cookie. Perfect for satisfying your chocolate cravings!

Red Velvet Cookies

Ingredients:

For the Cookies:

- **1 cup (2 sticks) unsalted butter**, at room temperature
- **1 cup granulated sugar**
- **1/2 cup packed brown sugar**
- **1 large egg**
- **1 tablespoon red food coloring** (gel or liquid)
- **1 tablespoon cocoa powder** (unsweetened)
- **1 teaspoon vanilla extract**
- **2 1/4 cups all-purpose flour**
- **1 teaspoon baking powder**
- **1/2 teaspoon baking soda**
- **1/4 teaspoon salt**

For the Cream Cheese Frosting (Optional):

- **4 oz cream cheese**, at room temperature
- **1/4 cup unsalted butter**, at room temperature
- **1 1/2 cups powdered sugar**
- **1 teaspoon vanilla extract**

Instructions:

1. **Preheat Oven**: Preheat your oven to 350°F (175°C). Line baking sheets with parchment paper or silicone baking mats.
2. **Cream Butter and Sugars**: In a large bowl, beat the butter, granulated sugar, and brown sugar together until light and fluffy.
3. **Add Egg, Food Coloring, and Cocoa Powder**: Beat in the egg, red food coloring, cocoa powder, and vanilla extract until well combined. The red food coloring will give the cookies their signature color.
4. **Combine Dry Ingredients**: In another bowl, whisk together the flour, baking powder, baking soda, and salt.
5. **Mix Dry Ingredients with Wet Ingredients**: Gradually add the dry ingredients to the butter mixture, mixing until just combined.
6. **Form Cookies**: Drop rounded tablespoons of dough onto the prepared baking sheets, spacing them about 2 inches apart. Flatten the dough slightly with the back of a spoon or your fingers if you prefer a more uniform shape.
7. **Bake**: Bake for 10-12 minutes, or until the edges are lightly golden and the centers are set. The cookies will firm up as they cool.
8. **Cool**: Allow the cookies to cool on the baking sheets for a few minutes before transferring them to a wire rack to cool completely.
9. **Optional Cream Cheese Frosting**: While the cookies are cooling, prepare the frosting. In a medium bowl, beat the cream cheese and butter together until smooth. Gradually add the powdered sugar and vanilla extract, beating until well combined and fluffy.

10. **Frost Cookies (Optional)**: Once the cookies are completely cooled, spread or pipe the cream cheese frosting onto the cookies.

These Red Velvet Cookies offer the classic flavors of red velvet cake in a convenient cookie form, with the option of adding a creamy, tangy cream cheese frosting for extra indulgence. Enjoy them as a festive treat or for any special occasion!

Hibiscus Orange Cookies

Ingredients:

For the Cookies:

- **1 cup (2 sticks) unsalted butter**, at room temperature
- **1 cup granulated sugar**
- **1/2 cup packed brown sugar**
- **1 large egg**
- **1 teaspoon vanilla extract**
- **1 tablespoon orange zest** (from about 1 orange)
- **1/4 cup fresh orange juice** (from about 1 orange)
- **2 1/4 cups all-purpose flour**
- **1 teaspoon baking powder**
- **1/2 teaspoon baking soda**
- **1/4 teaspoon salt**
- **1 tablespoon dried hibiscus petals**, finely crushed (or hibiscus powder)

For the Glaze (Optional):

- **1 cup powdered sugar**
- **2-3 tablespoons orange juice**
- **1 teaspoon orange zest**

Instructions:

1. **Preheat Oven**: Preheat your oven to 350°F (175°C). Line baking sheets with parchment paper or silicone baking mats.
2. **Cream Butter and Sugars**: In a large bowl, beat the butter, granulated sugar, and brown sugar together until light and fluffy.
3. **Add Egg and Flavorings**: Beat in the egg, vanilla extract, orange zest, and orange juice until well combined.
4. **Combine Dry Ingredients**: In another bowl, whisk together the flour, baking powder, baking soda, salt, and crushed dried hibiscus petals (or hibiscus powder).
5. **Mix Dry Ingredients with Wet Ingredients**: Gradually add the dry ingredients to the butter mixture, mixing until just combined.
6. **Form Cookies**: Drop rounded tablespoons of dough onto the prepared baking sheets, spacing them about 2 inches apart. Flatten each dough ball slightly with the back of a spoon or your fingers.
7. **Bake**: Bake for 10-12 minutes, or until the edges are lightly golden and the centers are set. The cookies will firm up as they cool.
8. **Cool**: Allow the cookies to cool on the baking sheets for a few minutes before transferring them to a wire rack to cool completely.
9. **Optional Glaze**: If using a glaze, whisk together the powdered sugar, orange juice, and orange zest until smooth. Drizzle the glaze over the cooled cookies.

These Hibiscus Orange Cookies feature a lovely balance of citrus and floral flavors, with a soft and chewy texture. The optional glaze adds a touch of sweetness and extra orange flavor, making them a refreshing and unique treat.

Gingerbread Whoopie Pies

Ingredients:

For the Gingerbread Cookies:

- **1/2 cup (1 stick) unsalted butter**, at room temperature
- **1/2 cup granulated sugar**
- **1/2 cup packed brown sugar**
- **1 large egg**
- **1/2 cup molasses**
- **2 1/4 cups all-purpose flour**
- **1 teaspoon baking soda**
- **1 tablespoon ground ginger**
- **1 tablespoon ground cinnamon**
- **1/2 teaspoon ground cloves**
- **1/4 teaspoon ground nutmeg**
- **1/4 teaspoon salt**

For the Filling:

- **1/2 cup (1 stick) unsalted butter**, at room temperature
- **1 cup powdered sugar**
- **4 oz cream cheese**, at room temperature
- **1 teaspoon vanilla extract**
- **1/2 teaspoon ground cinnamon**

Instructions:

1. **Preheat Oven**: Preheat your oven to 350°F (175°C). Line baking sheets with parchment paper or silicone baking mats.
2. **Make the Gingerbread Cookies**:
    - In a large bowl, cream together the butter, granulated sugar, and brown sugar until light and fluffy.
    - Beat in the egg and molasses until well combined.
    - In another bowl, whisk together the flour, baking soda, ground ginger, ground cinnamon, ground cloves, ground nutmeg, and salt.
    - Gradually add the dry ingredients to the butter mixture, mixing until just combined.
3. **Form and Bake Cookies**:
    - Drop rounded tablespoons of dough onto the prepared baking sheets, spacing them about 2 inches apart.
    - Flatten each dough ball slightly with the back of a spoon or your fingers.
    - Bake for 8-10 minutes, or until the edges are set and the cookies are firm.
    - Allow the cookies to cool on the baking sheets for a few minutes before transferring them to a wire rack to cool completely.
4. **Prepare the Filling**:

- In a medium bowl, beat the butter until creamy.
- Gradually add the powdered sugar and beat until smooth.
- Mix in the cream cheese, vanilla extract, and ground cinnamon until well combined.

5. **Assemble the Whoopie Pies**:
   - Once the cookies have cooled completely, spread a generous amount of the filling on the flat side of one cookie and top with another cookie, pressing gently to sandwich them together.

These Gingerbread Whoopie Pies are soft, spiced, and filled with a creamy, slightly tangy filling that complements the gingerbread perfectly. They're perfect for holiday treats or any time you want to enjoy a festive and flavorful dessert!

Peanut Butter Pretzel Cookies

Ingredients:

For the Cookies:

- **1 cup (2 sticks) unsalted butter**, at room temperature
- **1 cup creamy peanut butter**
- **1 cup granulated sugar**
- **1/2 cup packed brown sugar**
- **1 large egg**
- **1 teaspoon vanilla extract**
- **2 1/4 cups all-purpose flour**
- **1 teaspoon baking soda**
- **1/2 teaspoon baking powder**
- **1/4 teaspoon salt**
- **1 cup pretzel pieces** (broken into small chunks)

For the Topping (Optional):

- **1/2 cup additional pretzel pieces** (for pressing on top of cookies before baking)
- **Sea salt** (for sprinkling on top)

Instructions:

1. **Preheat Oven**: Preheat your oven to 350°F (175°C). Line baking sheets with parchment paper or silicone baking mats.
2. **Cream Butter, Peanut Butter, and Sugars**: In a large bowl, beat the butter, peanut butter, granulated sugar, and brown sugar together until light and fluffy.
3. **Add Egg and Vanilla**: Beat in the egg and vanilla extract until well combined.
4. **Combine Dry Ingredients**: In another bowl, whisk together the flour, baking soda, baking powder, and salt.
5. **Mix Dry Ingredients with Wet Ingredients**: Gradually add the dry ingredients to the butter mixture, mixing until just combined.
6. **Fold in Pretzel Pieces**: Gently fold in the pretzel pieces, being careful not to overmix.
7. **Form Cookies**: Drop rounded tablespoons of dough onto the prepared baking sheets, spacing them about 2 inches apart. For a more uniform appearance, you can roll the dough into balls and then flatten them slightly with the back of a spoon.
8. **Add Topping**: If desired, gently press a few additional pretzel pieces onto the top of each cookie before baking. You can also sprinkle a small pinch of sea salt on top for extra flavor.
9. **Bake**: Bake for 10-12 minutes, or until the edges are lightly golden and the centers are set. The cookies will firm up as they cool.
10. **Cool**: Allow the cookies to cool on the baking sheets for a few minutes before transferring them to a wire rack to cool completely.

These Peanut Butter Pretzel Cookies offer a delicious blend of creamy peanut butter and crunchy pretzels, with a hint of saltiness that enhances the flavor. They're perfect for snacking or sharing with friends and family!

Nutty Biscotti

Ingredients:

- **1 cup granulated sugar**
- **1/2 cup unsalted butter**, melted
- **3 large eggs**
- **1 teaspoon vanilla extract**
- **2 1/2 cups all-purpose flour**
- **1 teaspoon baking powder**
- **1/4 teaspoon salt**
- **1 cup chopped nuts** (e.g., almonds, walnuts, hazelnuts, or pistachios, toasted if desired)
- **1/2 cup mini chocolate chips** (optional, for extra flavor)

Instructions:

1. **Preheat Oven**: Preheat your oven to 350°F (175°C). Line a baking sheet with parchment paper or a silicone baking mat.
2. **Mix Wet Ingredients**: In a large bowl, whisk together the granulated sugar, melted butter, eggs, and vanilla extract until well combined.
3. **Combine Dry Ingredients**: In another bowl, whisk together the flour, baking powder, and salt.
4. **Mix Wet and Dry Ingredients**: Gradually add the dry ingredients to the wet ingredients, mixing until just combined.
5. **Add Nuts and Optional Chocolate Chips**: Fold in the chopped nuts and mini chocolate chips, if using.
6. **Shape Dough**: Divide the dough in half and shape each half into a log about 12 inches long and 2 inches wide on the prepared baking sheet. The logs will spread and flatten as they bake, so space them accordingly.
7. **Bake First Time**: Bake the logs for 25-30 minutes, or until golden brown and firm to the touch.
8. **Cool and Slice**: Allow the logs to cool on the baking sheet for about 10 minutes. Transfer the logs to a cutting board and slice them diagonally into 1/2-inch to 1-inch wide pieces.
9. **Bake Again**: Place the sliced biscotti cut-side up on the baking sheet and bake for an additional 10-15 minutes, or until the biscotti are crisp and golden brown.
10. **Cool**: Allow the biscotti to cool completely on a wire rack. They will continue to harden as they cool.

These Nutty Biscotti are perfect for enjoying with your favorite hot beverage, offering a delightful crunch and nutty flavor in every bite. They also make a great homemade gift for friends and family!

Honey Walnut Cookies

Ingredients:

- **1 cup (2 sticks) unsalted butter**, at room temperature
- **1 cup granulated sugar**
- **1/2 cup packed brown sugar**
- **1/2 cup honey**
- **1 large egg**
- **1 teaspoon vanilla extract**
- **2 1/4 cups all-purpose flour**
- **1 teaspoon baking powder**
- **1/2 teaspoon baking soda**
- **1/4 teaspoon salt**
- **1 cup chopped walnuts** (toasted if desired for extra flavor)

For the Topping (Optional):

- **1/4 cup honey** (for drizzling)
- **1/4 cup chopped walnuts** (for sprinkling)

Instructions:

1. **Preheat Oven**: Preheat your oven to 350°F (175°C). Line baking sheets with parchment paper or silicone baking mats.
2. **Cream Butter and Sugars**: In a large bowl, beat the butter, granulated sugar, and brown sugar together until light and fluffy.
3. **Add Honey, Egg, and Vanilla**: Beat in the honey, egg, and vanilla extract until well combined.
4. **Combine Dry Ingredients**: In another bowl, whisk together the flour, baking powder, baking soda, and salt.
5. **Mix Dry Ingredients with Wet Ingredients**: Gradually add the dry ingredients to the butter mixture, mixing until just combined.
6. **Fold in Walnuts**: Gently fold in the chopped walnuts.
7. **Form Cookies**: Drop rounded tablespoons of dough onto the prepared baking sheets, spacing them about 2 inches apart. Flatten each dough ball slightly with the back of a spoon if you prefer a more uniform shape.
8. **Bake**: Bake for 10-12 minutes, or until the edges are lightly golden and the centers are set. The cookies will firm up as they cool.
9. **Cool**: Allow the cookies to cool on the baking sheets for a few minutes before transferring them to a wire rack to cool completely.
10. **Optional Topping**: Once the cookies are completely cool, drizzle them with additional honey and sprinkle with extra chopped walnuts for added flavor and a decorative touch.

These Honey Walnut Cookies are a wonderful blend of sweet and nutty flavors, with a soft and chewy texture. They're perfect for a comforting snack or as a special treat to share with friends and family!

Pumpkin Chocolate Chip Cookies

Ingredients:

- **1 cup (2 sticks) unsalted butter**, at room temperature
- **1 cup granulated sugar**

- 1/2 cup packed brown sugar
- 1 cup canned pumpkin puree (not pumpkin pie filling)
- 1 large egg
- 1 teaspoon vanilla extract
- 2 1/4 cups all-purpose flour
- 1 teaspoon baking soda
- 1/2 teaspoon baking powder
- 1/2 teaspoon ground cinnamon
- 1/4 teaspoon ground nutmeg
- 1/4 teaspoon ground ginger
- 1/4 teaspoon salt
- 1 cup semi-sweet chocolate chips

Instructions:

1. **Preheat Oven**: Preheat your oven to 350°F (175°C). Line baking sheets with parchment paper or silicone baking mats.
2. **Cream Butter and Sugars**: In a large bowl, beat the butter, granulated sugar, and brown sugar together until light and fluffy.
3. **Add Pumpkin, Egg, and Vanilla**: Beat in the pumpkin puree, egg, and vanilla extract until well combined.
4. **Combine Dry Ingredients**: In another bowl, whisk together the flour, baking soda, baking powder, cinnamon, nutmeg, ginger, and salt.
5. **Mix Dry Ingredients with Wet Ingredients**: Gradually add the dry ingredients to the butter mixture, mixing until just combined.
6. **Fold in Chocolate Chips**: Gently fold in the chocolate chips.
7. **Form Cookies**: Drop rounded tablespoons of dough onto the prepared baking sheets, spacing them about 2 inches apart. The dough will spread a little during baking.
8. **Bake**: Bake for 12-15 minutes, or until the edges are lightly golden and the centers are set. The cookies will firm up as they cool.
9. **Cool**: Allow the cookies to cool on the baking sheets for a few minutes before transferring them to a wire rack to cool completely.

These Pumpkin Chocolate Chip Cookies are soft, spiced, and loaded with chocolate chips, making them a perfect treat for the fall season or any time you crave a delicious and comforting cookie. Enjoy them with a cup of coffee or tea!

Cinnamon Sugar Stars

Ingredients:

For the Cookies:

- 2 1/2 cups all-purpose flour

- 1 teaspoon baking powder
- 1/4 teaspoon salt
- **1 cup (2 sticks) unsalted butter**, at room temperature
- 1 cup granulated sugar
- 1 large egg
- 1 teaspoon vanilla extract

For the Cinnamon Sugar Coating:

- 1/4 cup granulated sugar
- 1 tablespoon ground cinnamon

Instructions:

1. **Preheat Oven**: Preheat your oven to 350°F (175°C). Line baking sheets with parchment paper or silicone baking mats.
2. **Combine Dry Ingredients**: In a medium bowl, whisk together the flour, baking powder, and salt. Set aside.
3. **Cream Butter and Sugar**: In a large bowl, beat the butter and sugar together until light and fluffy.
4. **Add Egg and Vanilla**: Beat in the egg and vanilla extract until well combined.
5. **Mix Dry Ingredients with Wet Ingredients**: Gradually add the dry ingredients to the butter mixture, mixing until just combined.
6. **Chill Dough**: Divide the dough in half, wrap in plastic wrap, and chill in the refrigerator for at least 1 hour or until firm. Chilling the dough makes it easier to roll out and cut.
7. **Prepare Cinnamon Sugar Coating**: In a small bowl, mix together the granulated sugar and ground cinnamon. Set aside.
8. **Roll and Cut Dough**: On a lightly floured surface, roll out one portion of the chilled dough to about 1/8 inch thickness. Use a star-shaped cookie cutter (or any other shape you like) to cut out cookies.
9. **Coat with Cinnamon Sugar**: Dip the cookie cutters into the cinnamon sugar mixture before cutting out each cookie to coat the edges with sugar. Place the cut-out cookies on the prepared baking sheets.
10. **Bake**: Bake for 8-10 minutes, or until the edges are lightly golden. The cookies will firm up as they cool.
11. **Cool**: Allow the cookies to cool on the baking sheets for a few minutes before transferring them to a wire rack to cool completely.

These Cinnamon Sugar Stars are a wonderful combination of buttery cookies with a sweet and spicy cinnamon sugar coating. They're perfect for holiday celebrations, gift-giving, or just a fun baking project!

Maple Bacon Cookies

Ingredients:

For the Cookies:

- 6 slices of bacon
- **1 cup (2 sticks) unsalted butter**, at room temperature

- 1 cup granulated sugar
- 1/2 cup packed brown sugar
- 1 large egg
- 1/2 cup pure maple syrup
- 1 teaspoon vanilla extract
- 2 1/4 cups all-purpose flour
- 1 teaspoon baking powder
- 1/2 teaspoon baking soda
- 1/4 teaspoon salt

For the Maple Glaze (Optional):

- 1 cup powdered sugar
- 2-3 tablespoons pure maple syrup
- 1/2 teaspoon vanilla extract

Instructions:

1. **Cook Bacon**: Cook the bacon in a skillet over medium heat until crisp. Remove the bacon from the skillet and drain on paper towels. Once cooled, crumble the bacon into small pieces. Reserve a small amount of bacon grease for adding to the dough if desired.
2. **Preheat Oven**: Preheat your oven to 350°F (175°C). Line baking sheets with parchment paper or silicone baking mats.
3. **Cream Butter and Sugars**: In a large bowl, beat the butter, granulated sugar, and brown sugar together until light and fluffy.
4. **Add Egg, Maple Syrup, and Vanilla**: Beat in the egg, maple syrup, and vanilla extract until well combined.
5. **Combine Dry Ingredients**: In another bowl, whisk together the flour, baking powder, baking soda, and salt.
6. **Mix Dry Ingredients with Wet Ingredients**: Gradually add the dry ingredients to the butter mixture, mixing until just combined. Fold in the crumbled bacon. If you reserved bacon grease, you can add a teaspoon or two for extra flavor.
7. **Form Cookies**: Drop rounded tablespoons of dough onto the prepared baking sheets, spacing them about 2 inches apart. Flatten each dough ball slightly with the back of a spoon or your fingers.
8. **Bake**: Bake for 10-12 minutes, or until the edges are lightly golden and the centers are set. The cookies will firm up as they cool.
9. **Cool**: Allow the cookies to cool on the baking sheets for a few minutes before transferring them to a wire rack to cool completely.
10. **Optional Maple Glaze**: While the cookies are cooling, prepare the glaze by whisking together the powdered sugar, maple syrup, and vanilla extract until smooth. Drizzle the glaze over the cooled cookies for added sweetness and maple flavor.

These Maple Bacon Cookies offer a wonderful blend of sweet and savory flavors with a delightful crunch from the bacon. They're perfect for those who enjoy unique and gourmet cookie recipes!

Tiramisu Cookies

Ingredients:

For the Cookies:

- 1 1/2 cups all-purpose flour
- 1/2 teaspoon baking powder

- 1/4 teaspoon salt
- 1/2 cup unsalted butter, room temperature
- 1/2 cup granulated sugar
- 1/2 cup brown sugar, packed
- 1 large egg
- 1 teaspoon vanilla extract
- 1/4 cup strong brewed coffee, cooled
- 1/2 cup mascarpone cheese

For the Coating:

- 1/2 cup granulated sugar
- 1 tablespoon cocoa powder
- 1 tablespoon instant espresso powder

For the Filling (Optional):

- 1/2 cup mascarpone cheese
- 1/4 cup powdered sugar
- 1/2 teaspoon vanilla extract

Instructions:

1. **Preheat Oven:** Preheat your oven to 350°F (175°C) and line a baking sheet with parchment paper.
2. **Prepare Dry Ingredients:** In a medium bowl, whisk together the flour, baking powder, and salt. Set aside.
3. **Cream Butter and Sugars:** In a large bowl, beat the butter, granulated sugar, and brown sugar together until creamy and light. This should take about 2-3 minutes.
4. **Add Egg and Vanilla:** Beat in the egg and vanilla extract until well combined.
5. **Incorporate Coffee and Mascarpone:** Mix in the cooled coffee and mascarpone cheese until smooth.
6. **Combine Dry and Wet Ingredients:** Gradually add the dry ingredients to the wet ingredients, mixing until just combined. The dough should be slightly sticky.
7. **Shape Cookies:** Scoop about 1 tablespoon of dough and roll it into a ball. Place it on the prepared baking sheet. Flatten each ball slightly with the bottom of a glass or your hand.
8. **Coat Cookies:** In a small bowl, mix the granulated sugar, cocoa powder, and instant espresso powder. Roll each cookie in this mixture before placing it back on the baking sheet.
9. **Bake:** Bake in the preheated oven for 10-12 minutes, or until the edges are golden brown. The centers will still be soft. Allow the cookies to cool on the baking sheet for a few minutes before transferring them to a wire rack to cool completely.
10. **Optional Filling:** If desired, mix the mascarpone cheese, powdered sugar, and vanilla extract in a bowl until smooth. Once the cookies are completely cooled, spread or pipe a

small amount of this filling onto the bottom of half of the cookies and sandwich them with the remaining cookies.

Tips:

- **Coffee**: Use a strong brew for the best flavor. Espresso or a dark roast works well.
- **Mascarpone Cheese**: Make sure it's at room temperature for easier mixing.
- **Cooling**: Allow the cookies to cool completely before filling to avoid melting the mascarpone filling.

Enjoy your tiramisu cookies with a nice cup of coffee or tea!

Cream Cheese Sugar Cookies

Ingredients:

- 2 1/2 cups all-purpose flour
- 1 teaspoon baking powder
- 1/4 teaspoon salt

- 1/2 cup unsalted butter, room temperature
- 1/2 cup cream cheese, room temperature
- 1 cup granulated sugar
- 1 large egg
- 1 teaspoon vanilla extract

Instructions:

1. **Preheat Oven:** Preheat your oven to 350°F (175°C). Line a baking sheet with parchment paper or a silicone baking mat.
2. **Prepare Dry Ingredients:** In a medium bowl, whisk together the flour, baking powder, and salt. Set aside.
3. **Cream Butter, Cream Cheese, and Sugar:** In a large bowl, beat the butter, cream cheese, and granulated sugar together until light and fluffy. This should take about 2-3 minutes.
4. **Add Egg and Vanilla:** Beat in the egg and vanilla extract until fully incorporated.
5. **Mix Dry Ingredients:** Gradually add the dry ingredients to the wet ingredients, mixing until just combined. Be careful not to overmix.
6. **Shape Cookies:** Scoop out rounded tablespoons of dough and place them on the prepared baking sheet. Flatten each ball slightly with the bottom of a glass or your hand.
7. **Bake:** Bake for 10-12 minutes, or until the edges are just starting to turn golden. The centers should still be soft.
8. **Cool:** Allow the cookies to cool on the baking sheet for 5 minutes before transferring them to a wire rack to cool completely.

Optional Frosting:

If you'd like to add frosting to your cookies, here's a simple recipe:

Ingredients for Frosting:

- 1/2 cup unsalted butter, room temperature
- 1 1/2 cups powdered sugar
- 2 tablespoons cream cheese, room temperature
- 1-2 tablespoons milk or cream
- 1 teaspoon vanilla extract

Instructions for Frosting:

1. **Beat Ingredients:** In a medium bowl, beat the butter and cream cheese together until smooth. Gradually add the powdered sugar, mixing on low speed until incorporated.
2. **Add Milk and Vanilla:** Mix in the milk (or cream) and vanilla extract. Beat until the frosting is smooth and spreadable. If the frosting is too thick, add a little more milk; if too thin, add more powdered sugar.

3. **Frost Cookies:** Once the cookies are completely cooled, spread or pipe the frosting onto them. Decorate as desired.

Enjoy your cream cheese sugar cookies with or without frosting—they're delicious either way!

Choco-Peanut Butter Swirl Cookies

Ingredients:

For the Cookie Dough:

- 1 1/2 cups all-purpose flour
- 1/2 teaspoon baking soda
- 1/4 teaspoon salt
- 1/2 cup unsalted butter, room temperature
- 1/2 cup creamy peanut butter (not natural)
- 1/2 cup granulated sugar
- 1/2 cup packed brown sugar
- 1 large egg
- 1 teaspoon vanilla extract
- 1/2 cup semi-sweet chocolate chips or chunks

For the Peanut Butter Swirl:

- 1/4 cup creamy peanut butter (not natural)
- 2 tablespoons powdered sugar (optional, for added sweetness)

Instructions:

1. **Preheat Oven:** Preheat your oven to 350°F (175°C). Line a baking sheet with parchment paper or a silicone baking mat.
2. **Prepare Dry Ingredients:** In a medium bowl, whisk together the flour, baking soda, and salt. Set aside.
3. **Cream Butter and Sugars:** In a large bowl, beat the butter, peanut butter, granulated sugar, and brown sugar together until light and fluffy, about 2-3 minutes.
4. **Add Egg and Vanilla:** Beat in the egg and vanilla extract until fully incorporated.
5. **Incorporate Dry Ingredients:** Gradually add the dry ingredients to the wet ingredients, mixing until just combined. Fold in the chocolate chips or chunks.
6. **Prepare Peanut Butter Swirl:** In a small bowl, mix the creamy peanut butter with the powdered sugar (if using) until smooth. This makes it easier to swirl.
7. **Shape and Swirl Cookies:** Scoop tablespoon-sized portions of dough onto the prepared baking sheet. Drop a small dollop of the peanut butter mixture onto each dough ball. Use a toothpick or a knife to gently swirl the peanut butter into the cookie dough. Be careful not to over-mix; you want to create a marbled effect.
8. **Bake:** Bake in the preheated oven for 10-12 minutes, or until the edges are golden brown. The centers will still be soft. Allow the cookies to cool on the baking sheet for 5 minutes before transferring them to a wire rack to cool completely.

Tips:

- **Peanut Butter**: Use creamy peanut butter for a smoother swirl. Natural peanut butter can be too oily and might not swirl as well.
- **Swirling**: The key to a good swirl is to not over-mix. You want to see both the chocolate and peanut butter in the finished cookie.
- **Storage**: Store the cookies in an airtight container at room temperature for up to a week, or freeze for longer storage.

These cookies are a fantastic combination of rich chocolate and creamy peanut butter, with each bite offering a delightful swirl of flavors. Enjoy!

Mango Coconut Cookies

Ingredients:

- 1 cup all-purpose flour
- 1/2 teaspoon baking powder
- 1/4 teaspoon salt

- 1/2 cup unsalted butter, room temperature
- 1/2 cup granulated sugar
- 1/4 cup packed brown sugar
- 1 large egg
- 1 teaspoon vanilla extract
- 1/2 cup dried mango, chopped into small pieces
- 1/2 cup shredded coconut (sweetened or unsweetened, according to preference)
- 1/4 cup chopped macadamia nuts (optional, for extra crunch)

Instructions:

1. **Preheat Oven:** Preheat your oven to 350°F (175°C). Line a baking sheet with parchment paper or a silicone baking mat.
2. **Prepare Dry Ingredients:** In a medium bowl, whisk together the flour, baking powder, and salt. Set aside.
3. **Cream Butter and Sugars:** In a large bowl, beat the butter, granulated sugar, and brown sugar together until light and fluffy, about 2-3 minutes.
4. **Add Egg and Vanilla:** Beat in the egg and vanilla extract until fully incorporated.
5. **Incorporate Dry Ingredients:** Gradually add the dry ingredients to the wet ingredients, mixing until just combined.
6. **Add Mango, Coconut, and Nuts:** Fold in the chopped dried mango, shredded coconut, and macadamia nuts (if using).
7. **Shape Cookies:** Scoop tablespoon-sized portions of dough onto the prepared baking sheet, spacing them about 2 inches apart. Flatten each dough ball slightly with the back of a spoon or your fingers.
8. **Bake:** Bake in the preheated oven for 10-12 minutes, or until the edges are golden brown and the centers are set. The cookies will continue to firm up as they cool.
9. **Cool:** Allow the cookies to cool on the baking sheet for 5 minutes before transferring them to a wire rack to cool completely.

Tips:

- **Dried Mango**: Use unsweetened dried mango for a more authentic flavor. If you use sweetened, you might want to reduce the amount of granulated sugar.
- **Coconut**: Shredded coconut can be sweetened or unsweetened based on your preference. If using sweetened, you might want to adjust the sugar content slightly.
- **Storage**: Store the cookies in an airtight container at room temperature for up to a week. They can also be frozen for up to 3 months.

Enjoy these tropical cookies with a cup of tea or coffee for a delightful treat!

Chili Chocolate Cookies

Ingredients:

- 1 3/4 cups all-purpose flour
- 1/2 cup unsweetened cocoa powder

- 1/2 teaspoon baking soda
- 1/4 teaspoon salt
- 1/2 teaspoon ground chili powder (adjust to taste)
- 1/2 teaspoon ground cinnamon
- 1/2 cup unsalted butter, room temperature
- 1/2 cup granulated sugar
- 1/2 cup packed brown sugar
- 1 large egg
- 1 teaspoon vanilla extract
- 1 cup semi-sweet chocolate chips or chunks
- 1/2 cup chopped nuts (optional, such as walnuts or pecans)

Instructions:

1. **Preheat Oven:** Preheat your oven to 350°F (175°C). Line a baking sheet with parchment paper or a silicone baking mat.
2. **Prepare Dry Ingredients:** In a medium bowl, whisk together the flour, cocoa powder, baking soda, salt, chili powder, and cinnamon. Set aside.
3. **Cream Butter and Sugars:** In a large bowl, beat the butter, granulated sugar, and brown sugar together until light and fluffy, about 2-3 minutes.
4. **Add Egg and Vanilla:** Beat in the egg and vanilla extract until fully incorporated.
5. **Incorporate Dry Ingredients:** Gradually add the dry ingredients to the wet ingredients, mixing until just combined. Fold in the chocolate chips or chunks and nuts if using.
6. **Shape Cookies:** Scoop tablespoon-sized portions of dough onto the prepared baking sheet, spacing them about 2 inches apart. Flatten each dough ball slightly with the back of a spoon or your fingers.
7. **Bake:** Bake in the preheated oven for 10-12 minutes, or until the edges are set and the centers are still slightly soft. The cookies will continue to firm up as they cool.
8. **Cool:** Allow the cookies to cool on the baking sheet for 5 minutes before transferring them to a wire rack to cool completely.

Tips:

- **Chili Powder**: Start with 1/2 teaspoon for a subtle heat. If you like it spicier, you can increase the amount. You can also experiment with different types of chili powder for varying heat levels and flavors.
- **Cocoa Powder**: Use high-quality unsweetened cocoa powder for the best chocolate flavor.
- **Storage**: Store cookies in an airtight container at room temperature for up to a week, or freeze for up to 3 months.

These cookies offer a deliciously spicy twist on classic chocolate cookies, making them perfect for those who love a little kick in their treats. Enjoy!

S'mores Macarons

Ingredients:

For the Macaron Shells:

- 1 cup (100g) almond flour
- 1 3/4 cups (200g) powdered sugar

- 3 large egg whites, at room temperature
- 1/4 teaspoon cream of tartar
- 1/4 cup (50g) granulated sugar
- 1/2 teaspoon vanilla extract
- 1 tablespoon cocoa powder (for chocolate flavor) or additional powdered sugar (for plain flavor)
- 1/4 teaspoon salt (optional, for extra flavor)

For the Graham Cracker Buttercream:

- 1/2 cup (115g) unsalted butter, room temperature
- 1 cup (120g) graham cracker crumbs
- 1 1/2 cups (190g) powdered sugar
- 1 tablespoon milk or cream
- 1/2 teaspoon vanilla extract

For the Marshmallow Filling:

- 1 cup (200g) granulated sugar
- 1/2 cup (120ml) water
- 2 large egg whites
- 1/4 teaspoon cream of tartar
- 1/2 teaspoon vanilla extract

For the Chocolate Ganache (Optional):

- 1/2 cup (120ml) heavy cream
- 1 cup (175g) semi-sweet chocolate chips or chopped chocolate

Instructions:

1. **Prepare Baking Sheets:** Line two baking sheets with parchment paper or silicone baking mats. Prepare a piping bag fitted with a round tip (about 1/2 inch) for piping the macaron shells.
2. **Sift Dry Ingredients:** In a medium bowl, sift together the almond flour, powdered sugar, and cocoa powder (if using). Set aside.
3. **Beat Egg Whites:** In a clean, dry bowl, beat the egg whites with an electric mixer until foamy. Add the cream of tartar and continue to beat until soft peaks form. Gradually add the granulated sugar, continuing to beat until stiff peaks form. Mix in the vanilla extract.
4. **Fold Dry Ingredients:** Gently fold the sifted dry ingredients into the egg white mixture. Fold until the batter flows like lava and forms a figure-eight when dropped from a spatula. Be careful not to overmix.
5. **Pipe Macaron Shells:** Transfer the macaron batter to the prepared piping bag. Pipe small circles (about 1.5 inches in diameter) onto the prepared baking sheets, spacing them about 1 inch apart. Tap the baking sheets gently on the counter to release any air bubbles.

6. **Rest Shells:** Let the piped shells rest at room temperature for 30-60 minutes, or until a skin forms and they are no longer sticky to the touch.
7. **Preheat Oven:** Preheat your oven to 300°F (150°C).
8. **Bake:** Bake the macaron shells for 15-20 minutes, or until they are set and easily lift off the parchment paper. Let them cool completely on the baking sheets.
9. **Prepare Graham Cracker Buttercream:** Beat the butter until creamy. Gradually add the graham cracker crumbs and powdered sugar, mixing until smooth. Add the milk and vanilla extract, and beat until the buttercream is light and fluffy.
10. **Prepare Marshmallow Filling:** In a medium saucepan, combine the granulated sugar and water. Heat over medium heat until the sugar dissolves and the mixture reaches 240°F (115°C) on a candy thermometer. While the sugar syrup is heating, beat the egg whites and cream of tartar until stiff peaks form.
    Once the sugar syrup reaches 240°F, slowly pour it into the beaten egg whites while continuing to beat. Beat until the mixture is cool and forms stiff peaks. Mix in the vanilla extract.
11. **Prepare Chocolate Ganache (Optional):** Heat the heavy cream in a small saucepan until just beginning to simmer. Pour over the chocolate in a bowl and let sit for 1-2 minutes. Stir until smooth and glossy. Let it cool slightly before using.
12. **Assemble Macarons:** Pipe a small amount of graham cracker buttercream onto the bottom of one macaron shell. Pipe a small amount of marshmallow filling on top of the buttercream. If using, pipe a small amount of chocolate ganache over the marshmallow. Sandwich with another macaron shell.
13. **Rest and Serve:** Let the assembled macarons rest in an airtight container in the refrigerator for 24 hours to allow the flavors to meld. Bring to room temperature before serving.

Enjoy these elegant s'mores macarons that pack all the delicious flavors of the classic campfire treat into a refined, bite-sized package!

Lemon Cream Sandwich Cookies

Ingredients:

For the Lemon Cookies:

- 1 3/4 cups all-purpose flour
- 1/2 teaspoon baking powder
- 1/4 teaspoon baking soda
- 1/4 teaspoon salt
- 1/2 cup unsalted butter, room temperature

- 1 cup granulated sugar
- 1 large egg
- 2 tablespoons fresh lemon juice
- 1 tablespoon lemon zest (from about 1 lemon)
- 1 teaspoon vanilla extract

For the Lemon Cream Filling:

- 1/2 cup unsalted butter, room temperature
- 1 cup powdered sugar
- 2 tablespoons fresh lemon juice
- 1 teaspoon lemon zest
- 1/2 teaspoon vanilla extract

Instructions:

1. **Preheat Oven:** Preheat your oven to 350°F (175°C). Line two baking sheets with parchment paper or silicone baking mats.
2. **Prepare Dry Ingredients:** In a medium bowl, whisk together the flour, baking powder, baking soda, and salt. Set aside.
3. **Cream Butter and Sugar:** In a large bowl, beat the butter and granulated sugar together until light and fluffy, about 2-3 minutes.
4. **Add Wet Ingredients:** Beat in the egg, lemon juice, lemon zest, and vanilla extract until fully incorporated.
5. **Incorporate Dry Ingredients:** Gradually add the dry ingredients to the wet ingredients, mixing until just combined. The dough will be soft.
6. **Shape Cookies:** Scoop out tablespoon-sized portions of dough and roll them into balls. Place them on the prepared baking sheets, spacing them about 2 inches apart. Flatten each ball slightly with the bottom of a glass or your fingers.
7. **Bake:** Bake in the preheated oven for 10-12 minutes, or until the edges are just starting to turn golden. The centers will still be soft. Let the cookies cool on the baking sheets for 5 minutes before transferring them to a wire rack to cool completely.
8. **Prepare Lemon Cream Filling:** In a medium bowl, beat the butter until creamy. Gradually add the powdered sugar, mixing on low speed until combined. Add the lemon juice, lemon zest, and vanilla extract. Beat until the filling is smooth and fluffy.
9. **Assemble Cookies:** Once the cookies are completely cooled, spread a generous amount of lemon cream filling on the bottom side of one cookie. Top with another cookie to form a sandwich. Press gently to spread the filling evenly.
10. **Serve:** Enjoy immediately or store the sandwich cookies in an airtight container at room temperature for up to a week.

Tips:

- **Lemon Zest**: Use fresh lemon zest for the best flavor. It adds a vibrant citrus note to the cookies and filling.

- **Butter Temperature**: Make sure your butter is at room temperature for both the cookies and the filling to ensure smooth and creamy mixtures.
- **Chilling Dough**: If the dough is too soft to handle, chill it in the refrigerator for about 30 minutes before baking.

These Lemon Cream Sandwich Cookies are a delightful combination of tangy lemon and sweet creaminess, perfect for any lemon lover!

www.ingramcontent.com/pod-product-compliance
Lightning Source LLC
LaVergne TN
LVHW081613060526
838201LV00054B/2238